GREEK POETRY
TRANSLATIONS

Dr. Marios Byron Raizis was educated at the University of Athens, Purdue, and New York University. He also holds diplomas from the Institute of World Affairs, the Air University and the University of Michigan. He has taught English at Purdue University, Wichita State University, Southern Illinois University, and the University of Athens.

Professor Raizis has authored, or edited, several scholarly books, articles, translations, and reviews. Since 1979 he has been Greek editor for *World Literature Today,* he is a member of the International Association of University Professors of English, the International Comparative Literature Association, the Byron Society, the Rydal Mount Association, the Modern Language Association of America, and the Modern Greek studies Association. He has been awarded prizes and grants from the Danforth Foundation, the National Endowment for the Humanities, the Academy of Athens, etc.

GREEK POETRY TRANSLATIONS

VIEWS - TEXTS - REVIEWS

M. Byron Raizis

EFSTATHIADIS GROUP

Efstathiadis Group S.A.
Agiou Athanasiou Street,
GR - 145 65 Anixi, Attikis

ISBN 960 226 194 3

© Efstathiadis Group S.A. 1993

Printed and bound in Greece by Efstathiadis Group S.A.

For my friend
Dr. Theodore Stephanides
and my
university students

BY THE SAME AUTHOR

Dionysios Solomos. New York: Twayne, 1972.

American Poets and the Greek Revolution, 1821-1828: A Study in Byronic Philhellenism. Thessaloniki: Institute of Balkan Studies, 1972 (with Alex Papas).

Greek Revolution and the American Muse: A Collection of Philhellenic Poetry. Thessaloniki: Institute of Balkan Studies, 1973.

The Literary Review: Greek Issue (Spring, 1973).

Essays and Studies from Professional Journals. Athens: Panhellenic Association of University Graduates in English, 1980.

Introduction to the Study of Literature. Athens: Panhellenic Association of University Graduates in English, 1980.

Ἀγγλόφωνη Φιλολογία: Συγκριτικές Μελέτες. Ἀθήνα: Κέδρος, 1981.

From Caucasus to Pittsburgh: The Prometheus Theme in British and American Poetry. Athens : Gnosis, 1982.

CONTENTS

VIEWS

INTRODUCTION

The Nature of Literary Translation

Most scholars who write about the art and "science" of translating literature do not fail to mention an Italian pun stating that "a translator is a traitor." That statement constitutes a paradox. Indeed, even the best of translations loses or betrays some important features of the original; but, on the other hand most people in the world know their Homer, Dante, Dostoyefsky, Kafka, Ibsen, Chekhov, and practically most literary giants, by means of translations. Paradoxically, the texts that, supposedly, "betray" the originals, have spread and preserved for posterity all that is beautiful and of perennial value in our civilization. In our day and age, even to imagine mastering so many languages—some of them dead—in order to be able to enjoy texts in their original articulation is an inconceivable impossibility for the majority of the world's educated.

Even in the past, the Christian Gospel, despite its "betrayal" by the Vulgate, reached the Europeans first, and then the inhabitants of the other continents, as a translation. In its Roman "habit" the Gospel inspired the millions, not in its original Greek. Much later, the *Communist Manifesto,* and other world-shaking texts, affected mankind in a translated form. Yes, a translation betrays, but it also preserves and promotes the essence of the original.

Another popular anecdote about literary translation is a French metaphor treating it as a woman (both are of feminine gender in French), a lover, of course. "The more beautiful, the more unfaithful," or its opposite: "The uglier, the more faithful." There is much truth in that French *jeux d'esprit.* A

12

very faithful, literal, *mot-à-mot,* translation is never a beautiful and convincing text in the target language. To faithfully reproduce all linguistic, structural, and formal features of a literary text into another language a translator would have to force the "capabilities" of the target tongue at times beyond its breaking point. To ignore form—what gives beauty and artistic quality to a message—and to focus solely on meaning amounts to reducing a work of art to a merely functional communication. While discussing the translation of poetry, ignoring literary form and concentrating only on words and what they mean is like noticing individual trees while failing to perceive the forest they belong to. The issue, then, is not how to translate *faithfully,* or how to translate *beautifully.* The issue is how to translate *both* beautifully *and* faithfully; how to achieve a happy *compromise* that does justice to the *message* of a text without betraying its *aesthetic integrity.* In absolute terms this may sound as an impossibility; in practical terms it is feasible if certain prerequisites are met. Some of these prerequisites are the following:

1. A translator of poetry must have a perfect command of his (her) mother tongue *and* of the target tongue.
2. A translator must be familiar with the literature, and especially the poetry, that has been produced in *both* languages.
3. Must be familiar with *both* cultures involved.
4. He must have an innate sense of rhythm and of all formalistic elements of poetry, or acquire them through practice. He must be imaginative, patient, and daring; he must also understand the dynamics of literary forms and of free verse.
5. He must have some poetic talent and sensibility; but he must never allow his own artistic mannerisms and "signatures" to manifest themselves in a translation whose original does not feature them.

Several major poets recreate, adapt, imitate, recast, paraphrase, interpret etc., original poetry rather than translate it. Their artistic personality—powerful and original as it normally is—often overwhelms the translator (i.e., scholar) in them who tries to work with all the data offered in the primary text. The *subjective* artist in his soul and mind eclipses the *objective* linguist. The poet selects what suits his taste, adds what is missing, and gives life to the new text by breathing his own creative spirit into it—at times becoming oblivious of the idiosyncratic habits that the patient and meticulous linguist never forgets. The result is not an objective recreation of a text; it is a subjective approximation, imitation, or whatever else you care to call it. In that category we certainly may place the late Robert Lowell, who would "imitate" a known text rather than translate it even freely, perhaps following the example of the great master, Ezra Pound. His artistic personality could not be checked and controlled in the process of confronting the challenges of inspiring and suggestive originals. On the other hand, a really great and objective translator is Richard Wilbur whose precise metrical translations of French Neoclassic plays in couplets are both scholarly and quite artistic.

Translators, who, as creative writers, do not like and avoid certain forms, genres, or types of compositions, should refrain from translating items which depend on them to be artistic entities. If they attempt to translate them, they are likely to ignore or violate pronounced features of the original with which they feel uncomfortable, in order to recast the material into forms, images, expressions, tones etc., that are *natural* to them. The result is, of course, a hybrid creation: a poem with *some* of the meaning and external features of the original, plus a form or other traits that are *alien* to it.

The famous Russian poet Vladimir Mayakofsky (1893-1930) composed only in rhythmical, metrical, or "stepped" lines, couplets etc.; yet most of his translators into Greek, trying to get his meaning right (or following the practice of irresponsible French or English translators), render his melodious and "structured" poems into free, uneven, and loose paragraphs. Now this is a "betrayal," not only a violation of form due to artistic exigency. It is also a gross historical inaccuracy when we know that the early Soviet regime did not allow or tolerate bourgeois modernist experimentations and *avant-garde* artistic forms in literature and most of the arts. When we present Mayakofsky of the 1920s writing free verse like a Greek half-a-century later, we also present him as our contemporary and a rebel against Party discipline. But he was neither, despite his disappointments. Alexis Parnis has rendered Mayakofsky poems precisely and accurately into Greek, no one else has, at least in aesthetic terms.

A similarly deplorable practice had condemned Kostes Palamas—one of Greece's celebrated poets—to eternal obscurity and anonymity. A master of traditional versification, form, diction, rhetoric, and cultural allusion, Palamas was stripped of what had made him an artist by aggressive and incompetent anglophone "translators" who reduced his musical octets, couplets, quatrains, sonnets etc., to unrhyming, free, loose, or outright prosaic lines. No wonder English-speaking readers had turned their backs to his poems until the publication of really poetic translations by the late George Katsimbalis and the still active Theodore Stephanides.

Such violations have also occurred freely in Greece. A certain "translator" of Lord Byron's *Childe Harold's Pilgrimage* (1818) turned its Spenserian stanzas (strophes of nine lines rhyming a, b, a, b, b, c, b, c, c) into Greek free verse paragraphs ranging in length all the way to over twenty loose lines. Of course, one may do that in prose (as Angelos Vlachos had done) and explain to his readers that this is a paraphrase in prose to carry the message—not the utterance—of the great poet to the Greeks. Few "translators" are so honest, though. Many take advantage of the Greek public's ignorance and serve them Byron and Mayakofsky in prose printed to look like free verse of the 1980s. Some foreigners do the same with classic or modern Greek verse, as we saw. "So it goes," as Kurt Vonnegut put it.

Going back over our list of prerequisites, we must emphasize that a translator of poetry should have a first-hand knowledge of the languages he works with, and not to translate translations. Translating on the basis of older translations may make the translator get the original *tone* wrong, miss the *connotation* of idioms and allusions, and perhaps create a parody. Now, if he is not familiar with the poetry in both tongues, he is not likely to find the right medium and exact equivalent for his text. For instance, one who does not know the importance of *blank verse* in English, or of the heroic couplet in the Cretan *Erotokritos,* may betray both of these measures and forms if he renders either of them in free verse, or in a metrical form that does not suit a sustained effort in the composition of narrative verse. Finally, a translator who cannot compose competent or 'correct' verse in his mother tongue, should think twice before attempting to turn foreign poems *as poems*—and not just as documents—into it. A successful translation is a good *compromise;* it is not a Herculean feat, or an act of martyrdom, so its maker should not feel arrogant.

Schools and Methods of Translation

When we distinguish translation methods we use descriptive adjectives like precise, literal, free, poetic, literary, and so on. Actually there are two main "philosophies" of translation, two diametrically different "schools," each advocating and practising its own method: *literal* or *free.* All other categories are but subdivisions of the two main attitudes, and they cover various parts of the spectrum that begins and ends with the two extremes.

Literal we call a translation whose primary purpose is the exact and accurate rendition of the meaning and form of one text into a target language. If this can be achieved through a

16

word by word (verbatim) substitution, so much the better. This method, which in olden times was widely used to translate speculative texts in prose (philosophy, theology, theory of law, criticism) tends to impose linguistic "straight jackets" on purely literary texts, since many linguistic mannerisms, grammatical and syntactical phenomena, and even formalistic and stylistic practices are not common or natural in any two tongues. In translating poetry, in particular, the literal method yields a text that cannot have artistic qualities, as it sounds contrived, with its unnatural mannerisms, unidiomatic usage, alien cultural allusions, unfamiliar forms, and so on. It follows then that a *literal* method is almost never used effectively in translating literature, and is out of the question in translating verse, since measures and versification schemes rarely correspond in two poetic compositions in two different tongues saying the same things in the same way. A Greek decapentasyllabic line cannot be matched by an English fifteen-syllable line—which is rarer than a four-leaf clover. A certain adjustment is in order. Similarly, lexical peculiarities, such as the economical wording of proverbs, their imagery, rhythm etc., may only be approximated by semantically analogous proverbs in the target language. For instance, "to call a spade, a spade," can only be rendered in Greek as εἶπε τά σῦκα, σῦκα καί τή σκάφη, σκάφη. Any attempt at saying in Greek εἶπε τό τσαπί, τσαπί, though it makes sense will be awkward or even ludicrous since that phrase is alien to Greek culture. By the same token, you cannot translate στό κάτω, κάτω τῆς γραφῆς as "at the bottom, bottom of the writing (scripture, letter etc.)," because that phrase does not constitute functional English, to say the least.

Free is a translation that conveys the meaning of the original into the target tongue by paying only *partial attention* to the details of the medium, or just the opposite: it respects the means (medium) at the expense of meaning. By contrast to the literal method, the free method invariably yields very readable, even beautiful texts in the target tongue. But the price is high: often a free translation carries only a *small fraction* of the features of the original. Often, the "picture" of the original that it gives us is inaccurate or even misleading. Cf, a prose translation of the *Iliad* in Victorian diction, or in contemporary diction and free verse.

Obviously the free translation method would be unsuitable for the rendition of legalistic or philosophical documents; as terms with precise shades of meaning could literally be mistranslated by widely used terms in the target tongue, which, however, have different connotations. For instance, the Greek phrase ἁρματωλοί καί κλέφτες, when freely rendered as "guerrillas and partisans"—which is more natural and common than the literal "armed men and thieves"—will actually connote communist sympathizers of the 1930s and later, rather than Christian anti-Turk irregulars of the 1820s. In cases like this the retention of the key word *Klepht* is in order (as Lord Byron had done), with a brief note explaining its special meaning.

Great care is needed when translating literature freely (liberally), to avoid making the natural expression in the target tongue a distant and, at times, discordant echo of the original. A very casual English expression such as "we had a couple of drinks together," does not exactly render something like εἴπιαμε δυό ποτηράκια (which implies *wine*), or εἴπιαμε δυό οὐζάκια, because drinking ouzo is normally accompanied by eating snack while sitting leisurely in chairs to chat and while the time away; whereas a couple of drinks at a bar, without any snacks, while standing or sitting on stools is a different social ritual than the Greek. Obviously, one has to avoid the extremes of both, literal and free, translations, and use judiciously elements from both to achieve a working balance, what we called a "happy compromise."

Extreme cases of free translations are sometimes what we mean by *paraphrase, adaptation,* and *imitation.* Though each of these terms is self-explanatory, we could attempt to define them here.

A *paraphrase* is a restatement of a text based on a re-wording, usually to make it more intelligible, and/or shorter; that is, "we say the same thing in different words." When paraphrase refers to a translation, its sense tends to be pejorative or deprecatory, since the quality and impact of a paraphrase are inferior to those of the standard, or original, text by definition. Some people would not hesitate to call a bad, an unfaithful, translation a paraphrase. An example of a mistranslation that could be considered a paraphrase of sorts is an American free version of Kypros Chrysanthis's fine sonnet «Λευκωσία», included in this book (in Greek and in my more precise translation). All stanzas of that lyric have been heavily "doctored," with a generous amount of additions that make it a new poem—not any longer Chrysanthis's—which, however, has too-irregular a rhyme scheme to be called a sonnet. In other words, both meaning and form have been violated. Compare its beginning in the original and in its two versions:

Γύρα θαμμάτων ὥρα καί πλημμύρα,	a
Λύχνων θυμητικῶν ροδάτη φλόγα,	b
κι ὦ Λευκωσία, τό δεῖλι ἐκορφολόγα	b
τόν οὐρανό σου σά θαυμάσια μοῖρα.	a

For miracles and a flood is the time,	a
Of commemorative lamps the rosy flames;	b
And, Lefkosia, the twilight frames	b
Your sky like a fate sublime.	a
	(mine)

This is the hour of miracles, *when the sea barks.*
The earth flames with memorial lamps *and darkens:*
Evening, nipping off the end-budds of your sky,
O Leukosia, like a splendid destiny.

(D. Posner)

One notices that despite the additions *(in italics)* and the omission of the poetic adjective ροδάτη (rosy), the second translation fails to achieve steady measures and the rhyme pattern (a, b, b, a) that the first one does. Yet, Mr. Posner is a good poet and renders the last two lines imaginatively. His work, however, is a strange hybrid, distantly related to Dr. Chrysanthis's original, either in terms of sound or of meaning.

An *imitation,* on the other hand, according to Robert Lowell, is an artistic re-creation of an original "made to ring right" for the imitator. This is hardly a translation, though. In all cases, a good imitation is freer and more subjective than even a "free" translation. Lowell's prose imitation of Aeschylus' poetic drama *Prometheus Bound* is quite an original and modern philosophical play of the late 1960s in America. Its concerns are existential and political rather than theological. An imitation is based on an older and prestigious text, or derives from it. It does not purport to be its translation.

An *adaptation* is often freer and more distantly related to an original than both, *imitation* and *paraphrase.* The process of adapting a text implies not only transferring its meaning from one medium into another, but, quite frequently, altering its genre, form, and other characteristics while retaining certain salient features. For instance, Albert Camus's adaptation as a French play of Dostoyefsky's Russian novel *The Possessed;* or the adaptation as a "musical," *My Fair Lady,* of George Bernard Shaw's comedy *Pygmalion.* In Greek we have numerous adaptations as juvenile literature of serious fiction in English, like Dickens's *David Copperfield,* and Swift's *Gulliver's Travels.* Celebrated are also Charles Lamb's prose adaptations for juveniles of Shakespeare's poetic dramas.

The terms *version* and *rendition* are also occasionally used in reference to translation. Both, it seems to me, are so general, vague, or broad in meaning, that, at best, imply a personal, subjective *interpretation* (or, exegesis) of a text, rather than a responsible and genuine translation of its meaning and form. Terrence Rattigan used the word *version* (meaning "free translation") in his play, *The Browning Version,* i.e. of a drama by Aeschylus.

It is unwise to advocate the use of only one method in translating poetry. It is far better for a translator to be flexible and to attempt a precise or a free translation—or even a recasting of the poem—depending on the special problems that each individual poem, or stanza, presents.

In general, in translating free verse it is possible to do a good job while remaining faithful to its literal meaning and lexical features, provided we make the necessary idiomatic, cultural, syntactical, and literary adjustments. That is, a precise translation is possible, desirable, and thus warranted in the case of compositions in free verse. This precision, however, by no means implies a verbatim rendition, line by line, image by image, etc. Even free verse is subject to the idiosyncracy and ethnic heritage that begot it, and these are not automatically transferable from tongue to tongue. Naturalness of utterance in the target language is a *sine qua non;* otherwise the translation has little, or no, literary merit. For example, the title of Dino Christianopoulos's poem «Ἀντιγόνης ὑπέρ Οἰδίποδος»—which reminds us of familiar classical orations, and is cleverly and perfectly Greek at all times—should be rendered as "Antigone's Defense of Oedipus," even in a precise translation. Anything more literal, for instance, "Antigone's Speech in Support of Oedipus," would sound verbose, and thus prosaic, pedantic, and unpoetic.

Again, in general, the translation of metrical lines of traditional and conventional verse forms and techniques presents greater and more problems than free verse. This is not an absolute truth, though. The reader will notice that a few stanzas of Solomos were turned into metrical and rhyming English verse without much ado.

Conventional poetic forms present difficulties through the technical and stylistic restrictions inherent in their forms. Also, standard stanzaic variations and rhyme schemes or

21

metrics impose limitations on the translator's choices of words and devices. We saw earlier in this Introduction that many translators of traditional compositions avoid or bypass these specific problems by ignoring form and rhyme demands, and by offering a precise lexical and semantic equivalence which carries the message. They also embellish the expression in the target language, and somehow control the length of lines to give the whole an impression of neatness and austerity that characterize "structured" verse forms.

This salutary practice satisfies the reader who is primarily interested in the *meaning* of a poem. Now, if the reader is sophisticated enough to want to know *how* (by what means) this meaning is conveyed, and turned into an artistic creation, then this practice seems inadequate. Many statements in the beautiful forms of Solomos, Palamas, or Sikelianos are not terribly original, profound, or impressive to a sophisticated foreign reader if they are presented stripped of the forms that made them poetry in the first place. The competent translator is called then to show the professional dexterity and skill of these poets in their use of appropriate stanzaic forms, types of compositions, patterns of rhymes, and all manner of artistic devices that create poetic effects—music with words, aura, atmosphere, synaesthesia, mystification, etc., that turn a text into a lyrical vibration, into a poem.

It is my firm belief that the translation of a Greek sonnet, an *ottava rima,* a quatrain, a couplet, should be an English sonnet, *ottava rima,* quatrain, and couplet respectively. Both languages borrowed, and developed, most of these forms from Italian poetry; both naturalized them, and in both artists articulated pretty much the same themes and concerns. It is an unpardonable sin to "translate" a rhyming and musical octave by Palamas into an unrhyming quatrain, or free verse paragraph, in British or American English, as has been done. Palamas wrote no *prose documents* in those cases; he wrote *poems.* He also wrote many essays, articles, and reviews, or stories, in prose. Does a "translator" have the right to reduce

22

even his poetry to prose? I think not. Strip a poem of its lyrical "vestments," and it gets reduced to a mere statement of questionable profundity and limited appeal.

To achieve a translation which is *precise in meaning* and *corresponding in form,* one has often to resort to *anaplasis, transposition, padding, omission, inversion,* and even *correction,* or adjustment, of figures of speech, imagery, and poetic diction. What should never be tampered with is *tone.* An altered *tone* changes a whole poem as surely and the use of different words does. I still remember the disappointment I shared with a German professor when we studied together an 'adaptation' of Rainer Maria Rilke's "Self-Portrait." That serious sonnet had been turned by an imaginative American into a melodious sonnet whose meaning was miles apart from Rilke's, on account of the translator's idiosyncratic manipulation of its tone.

By *anaplasis* we mean a remoulding, a recasting of the words, expressions, imagery etc., of the original into new and different but more naturally corresponding lexical features in the target tongue, when, *and only when,* the use of direct analogues does not yield poetic and idiomatic lines in the target language. In addition, the liberty taken with anaplasis demands a religious respect of fo ¬. Changing the lexical data, as well as the technical data, of an original will never result in a *translation,* as we saw earlier. Anaplasis was used by some translators of Solomos, Palamas, and some Cavafy, who had to solve the problem posed by the wealth of the Greek vocabulary (archaic, puristic, demotic, cultural, colloquial) and the demands of historical forms.

What a translator dreads to do is *omission,* its opposite *padding,* and *inversion.* Yet all three are inevitable in order to obtain meaning, rhyme, and form in English. One has to weigh very carefully the advantages of employing them, versus the disadvantages—the liberties taken with precision, lexical approximation, and overall rhetoric in a given text.

In certain cases (even in free verse) *padding* is mandatory to achieve a specific number of syllables or beats in the target tongue, and thus avoid hiatus in rhythm or unnaturally short lines to cause the desired effect. We often have to pad English lines that translate Greek ones containing several polysyllabic words which may be rendered into English by an equal number of monosyllabic words. For instance, the Greek σταυροδρόμι (four syllables) corresponds to the English "cross-roads" (two syllables); σιδερόφραχτος becomes two syllables (iron-clad). If these words are contained in deca-pentasyllabic demotic lines, the English version may come out with fewer than seven or eight syllables; to compose then ten-syllable English *blank verse*—the cultural equivalent to the fifteen-syllable Greek line—we have to add one, two, or more syllables—one or more words. If that is the case we should try to add suitable words whose addition will not interfere with the overall meaning and tone of the text. A knowledgeable translator can think of such 'innocent' or 'neutral' additions for his *padding*.

We must do the opposite, *omission,* when the items to be translated in one line or sentence are too many and awkward after the literal, *mot-à-mot,* translation. In that case we choose to omit the most 'innocent', 'colorless', or 'neutral' noun or adjective, particle or adverb, whose absence will not affect meaning, tone, mood. On the contrary, that omission should improve the translation in terms of rhythm and naturalness of expression. Kimon Friar has made very judicial uses of *omission* as well as of *padding* in his monumental translation of Kazantzakis's *Odyssey.* I have tried to follow his example—less expertly, I am afraid—in several of my translations here.

Inversion, the disruption of the normal word order in a sentence, is another dreaded and dangerous practice by translators. Widely used by anglophone poets up to the appearance of modern poetry (World War I), *inversion* was considered anathema by Ezra Pound who convinced his contemporaries of its offensiveness and obsolescence. Still, inversion was one of the commonest stylistic mannerisms in Romantic, Victorian, and most of Georgian poetry. Its use in the translation of poems by nineteenth-century Greeks should be tolerated to indicate, somehow, the historical period of traditional compositions, and to achieve metrics and forms that were common then. So "sublime fate" may be inverted to "fate sublime," which, of course, may sound offensive in a modern poem. Most of my metrical translations of conventional forms in this collection use inversion. I hope that they do not abuse it.

Corrections in the exact expression, or wording, may at times be in order. Example: the last line in the Chrysanthis sonnet we discussed earlier reads: π' ἀνθεῖ, ἀπ' τούς ξένους ἄν κι' ἐφυλλορόγα. The American version changed this completely, by introducing the image of Aphrodite, to: "Though her face lies wrinkled in a stranger's hand," which ignores the positive element, π' ἀνθεῖ. I first translated it faithfully as, "That's blooming, although it shed its leaves." Objective native speakers remarked to me then that it is self-contradictory, or incongruous, to say that something is blossoming or blooming—that is, flourishing—while it is losing its leaves, or had shed them up to that hour. So under the demands of logic, *I corrected* the line in English to mean that the wilting is over, and that now the animated abstraction is blooming: "That's blooming, no longer wilted by conquerors' tread," rather than "That's blooming, although wilted by conquerors' tread," that sounds illogical.

Transposition enables an imaginative translator to create artistic effects, and to avoid awkward or unnatural lines, by transposing a word, phrase, or line from its original place to a more natural one in the target tongue. Care, of course, should be taken to avoid altering the *context* of the two lines involved. Mr. Friar used transposition in his translation of the *Odyssey* as well as in many other texts. In rendering a quatrain, for example, line 2 may become line 3 or 4 in the translation provided there is a good reason for this change, that is, an aesthetic need may be satisfied without affecting the meaning significantly. Sometimes sophisticated or intricate uses of transposition achieve real miracles in the *anaplasis* of a line or stanza. Let us see some of the above-mentioned devices in practice by examining how I translated Solomos's impressive epigramme "To Psara," into an English lyric of equivalent power and impact, through the application of a reasonable amount of poetic license.

Στῶν Ψαρῶν τήν ὁλόμαυρη ράχη,	a
περπατώντας ἡ Δόξα μονάχη,	a
μελετᾶ τά λαμπρά παληκάρια	b
καί στήν κόμη στεφάνι φορεῖ,	c
γιναμένο ἀπό λίγα χορτάρια	b
πού 'χαν μείνει στήν ἔρημη γῆ.	c

On Psara's blackened, charred stone,	a
Glory silently walks all alone,	a
Meditating her sons' noble deeds;	b
And wears a wreath on her hair	c
Made of such few scattered weeds	b
On the desolate earth left to spare.	c

To begin with, the ten-syllable italianate line of the stately-moving Greek must be reduced to around eight in English, to avoid drastically altering its extremely appropriate rhythm by slowing it down. To achieve a similarly sombre mood through sound effects, I translated literally, or precisely, all lines to judge which one should be used as a *norm* suggesting a pattern for the rest of the poem, as it were. The fourth line, "And wears a wreath on her hair," appealed to me at once on account of its smooth and proper rhythm, accuracy, harmony, alliteration, and assonance. It was not difficult to adjust line sixth to make it rhyme with "hair":"On the desolate earth left (to spare)," by adding the two syllables "to spare"—a fortunate case of padding, since its neutrality of meaning does not change anything semantically, while removing a possible hiatus.

The second line, "Glory (silently) walks all alone," impressed me no less, on account of its melodious labials (l). The addition of the adverb "silently" achieved two important goals: First, it reinforced the l-sound effect effectively; and, second, it enriched the image of the allegorical figure of Glory walking in solemn steps, like a divine spirit, against the silence of eternity and of total desolation.

Line three had to be adjusted to fit the rhythm and rhyme pattern already established by the three successfully translated lines. So it became, "Meditating her sons' noble deeds," instead of the more literal, precise, but prosaic, "She meditates the brilliant (noble) brave (or young) warriors," which is quite awkward in English since warriors are, by definition, young and brave, and brilliant (distinguished, noble) because of their actions. The redundance that developed in the translation had to be checked and removed by omitting one of the adjectives implied in παληκάρια and merging it with λαμπρά. "Noble" sounded better than "brilliant" in this context, and by transposing it to qualify the actions (deeds) of the fighters, rather than the fighters themselves—not a significant change in meaning—I finally got that difficult line to suit the established scheme, as "Meditating her sons' noble deeds." That line made me take more liberties with the wording by Solomos. To avoid hiatus right after "Meditating," and to bring Glory closer to the heroic dead, I added the possessive "her" with its strong connotation of intimacy which actually strengthened Solomos's idea that those dead warriors are glorious.

"Deeds" is more impressive and poetic than "actions," and rhymes with "weeds" (χορτάρια); so I got my fifth line, too, by just adding the words "such" and "scattered," both of which are implied in the Greek and in the image it draws. Line one posed the greatest problems. The words "ridge" or "crest" (ράχη) could not rhyme with the correct and beautiful "alone," so a substitution was in order. Knowing the harsh, rocky terrain of that island, I realized at once that the word "stone" would somehow—not perfectly, I knew it—do as a substitute for "ridge" or "crest," without affecting the meaning significantly, since, instead of the *elevation* where the dead warriors lay (ράχη), I referred to the general *hardness* of the rocky ground by means of the word "stone," which did not contradict anything in the description of that impressive tableau. Finally, ὁλόμαυρη is a hard adjective to translate. The darkness and blackness it denotes are obviously the result of fighting and conflagration. It is the blackness caused by the burned powder of guns and muskets, and by the smoke of the fires put by the Turks. So the addition of the participle "charred" enhanced the meaning by suggesting how the island "blackened." In the process of translating this epigramme I applied, as we saw, some *padding, inversion, transposition* (i.e., transferred epithet), and one word *substitution*. The result contains about nine tenths of the lexical features of the original (imagery, personification etc.), plus 100% of the integrity of its form (the rhythm and economy of an epigramme).

The above process may be termed a "free translation," because of the lexical equivalents employed, despite the fact that it renders form and other technical details with absolute accuracy. If more liberties had been taken with its wording to achieve the epigramme prerequisites, the result would have to be an *anaplasis,* a drastic recasting of its data into the mould of its demanding form. I would perhaps consider as *anaplases* the two *ottava rima* stanzas of Solomos's "Lambros" included in this book. On the other hand, most of my other translations of free verse poems (and even of some metrical pieces) are obviously precise and faithful, as I never tried to absolutely anglicize or americanize them in terms of expression, allusion, and connotation, to avoid betraying the original. That does not mean that I was always successful, or that I am a seasoned translator. The fact, however, is that native speakers of English—creative writers and scholars of literature—approved of my efforts and recommended the publication of my translations to various academic magazines of quality.

TEXTS

The present body of Greek poems in my English translation does not constitute a complete or a formal anthology, and it does not claim to be one. It is a collection of translations that were published in various American, Canadian, and Greek quality magazines and other publications of literary scholarship or creative writing. A few more translations were added when the collection was compiled.

I am not presenting these texts as a representative sample of Modern Greek verse since the 1820s. I am presenting them as legitimate products of my academic and professional efforts at poetic translation. Since the poets, translators, critics, and professors who edited the magazines that featured them for the first time approved of my efforts, I am offering them to my English students, and to all anglophone lovers of poetry, as samples of what poetry translations may be to successfully meet the criteria of native speakers of English who are experts in the composition and translation of poetry.

Two are the greatest assets of this collection. First, it features George Seferis's last collection, *Three Secret Poems* (1966), in its entirety (minus the Greek original), all twenty-eight pieces of it, plus his very last composition, the resistance lyric "Against Whitethorns. . ." (1971). Second, it includes (bilingually) many celebrated poems by Dionysios Solomos —the Bard of Greek independence—and several more pieces in traditional and conventional verse forms, for the first time in correct and precise metrical English translations. Thus the student of literary translation will have the opportunity to observe and examine how rhyme schemes, stanzaic forms, and steady measures may be achieved, or approximated, in the target tongue.

Broadly speaking, these poems belong to two large categories. Those of traditional versification and historical forms, and those of free verse and looser forms.

The first category features various traditional compositions of Solomos—some in their entirety—including *ottava rima* stanzas, and many quatrains from his elegiac ode on Lord Byron's death. Sonnets and epigrams by John Gryparis, George Drosinis, Kostas Karyotakis, and John Polemis—all inspired by Lord Byron's death—a sonnet by Michael Stasinopoulos (former President of the Hellenic Republic), a sonnet by the Cypriot veteran Dr. Kypros Chrysanthis, and excerpts from two verse dramas by the late and great Nikos Kazantzakis complete the group of my metrical translations in historical forms.

A group of poems in free verse represents the work of Cypriot poets covering two successive generations: Manos Kralis, Petros Sophas, Yannis Papadopoulos, and Nadina Dimitriou—all of them still alive. These poems were chosen because they show different trends, techniques, and styles, all practiced in excellent demotic Greek.

The largest category includes compositions of Helladic poets in free verse. Apart from the already mentioned Nobel Prize Winner (1963) George Seferis, several fine lyrics by the veteran Nikephoros Vrettakos enrich this group, plus poems by the following poets (in alphabetical order): Takis Antoniou, Markos Avyeris, Nikos Aslanoglou, Dinos Christianopoulos Ares, Diktaios, Dimitris Doukaris, Philip Drakodiaides, Andreas Embirikos, Nikos Engonopoulos, Anestis Evangelou, Zoë Karelli, George Kotsiras, Kostes Kokorovits, T. Pittas, George Stoyannides, Panos Thasites, George Themelis, Takis Varvitsiotes, and Koula Yiokarini. Among them Varvitsiotes, Themelis, Thasites, Stoyannides, Karelli, Evangelou, Christianopoulos, and Aslanoglou represent the thriving poetic Muse of Northern Greece, especially of Salonica. I must emphasize here that the order of appearance of these artists' texts in the book was dictated by technical considerations, and it does not indicate a hierarchy of aesthetic or other values.

I express here my warmest thanks to all these poets and their publishers for allowing us to present samples of their works here. Special thanks are due to Mrs. Maro G. Seferis for her generosity; and to Mrs. Helen N. Kazantzakis's representative, the Honorable Undersecretary to the Presidency of the Cypriot Republic, Mr. Patroklos Stavrou, old friend and fellow student at the University of Athens.

Finally, sincere thanks to the editors of the aforementioned periodicals for having encouraged my efforts through publication, and for having allowed me to republish these poems in the present book: Professor Donald E. Stanford of Louisiana State University, Professor Rainer Schulte of Ohio University, Professor Charles Angoff of Fairleigh Dickinson University, Professor Frances M. Rippy of Ball State University, Professor Jacob Zilber of the University of British Columbia, Mr. Michael Bullock of the University of British Columbia, Professor Kostas Myrsiades of West Chester State College, Professor Stavros Deligiorgis of the University of Iowa, Professor Jim Clark of Vanderbilt University, Professor David Rogers of Seton Hall University, Mr. Dino Siotis of San Francisco; and, above all, Professor K. Mitsakis of the University of Athens, and Professor Ivar Ivask of the University of Oklahoma. Their friendship and support made this book possible.

Marios Byron Raizis
The University of Athens

TRADITIONAL POETRY

DIONYSIOS SOLOMOS

The Dream

My soul, goddess of beauty,
Listen to what I've dreamed:
With you I was one night,
All to me so splendid seemed.

We two walked together
In a garden full of fragrance,
All the stars shone brightly
And on them you kept your glance.

I was asking them, "Stars say
If among you there lies
One that shines from up there
Like my lovely lady's eyes?

Say whether you ever saw
On others such pretty hair?
Such an arm, such a limb,
An angelic vision fair?

* Such a figure full of beauty
* At once a question brings:
* 'If this creature is an angel
* Why is she lacking wings?' "

* I had spoken this way
* When before my very sight,
* Other girls appeared clad
* In the moon's silvery light.

* Holding hands they danced together,
* All of them, pretty and smart,
* Each one trying with fervor
* To win my heart.

ΔΙΟΝΥΣΙΟΣ ΣΟΛΩΜΟΣ

Τό Όνειρο

Άκου ἕν' ὄνειρο, ψυχή μου,
Καί τῆς ὀμορφιᾶς θεά·
Μοῦ ἐφαινότουν ὁπώς ἤμουν
Μετ' ἐσένα μία νυχτιά.

Σ' ἕνα ὡραῖο περιβολάκι
Περπατούσαμε μαζί·
Ὅλα ἐλάμπανε τ' ἀστέρια
Καί τά κοίταζες ἐσύ.

Ἐγώ τσὄλεα: Πέστε, ἀστέρια,
Εἶν' κανέν' ἀπό τ' ἐσᾶς,
Πού νά λάμπη ἀπό 'κει ἀπάνου
Σάν τά μάτια τῆς κυρᾶς;

Πέστε ἄν εἴδετε ποτέ σας
Σ' ἄλλη τέτοια ὡραῖα μαλλιά,
Τέτοιο χέρι, τέτοιο πόδι,
Τέτοια ἀγγελική θωριά;

* Τέτοιο σῶμα ὡραῖον ὁπ' ὅποιος
* Τό κοιτάζει εὐθύς ρωτᾶ:
* Ἄν εἶν' ἄγγελος ἐκεῖνος,
* Πῶς δέν ἔχει τά φτερά;

* Ὅ,τι εἶπα αὐτά τά λόγια,
* Μοῦ ἐφανήκανε ὀμπρός
* Ἄλλες κόρες στολισμένες
* Μέ τοῦ φεγγαριοῦ τό φῶς.

* Ἐχορεύανε πιασμένες
* Ἀπ' τά χέρια τά λευκά,
* Κι' ὅλες τους ἐπολεμοῦσαν
* Νά μοῦ πάρουν τήν καρδιά.

37

* Then I heard your lips say,
* As you were addressing me:
* "Do you like them? Tell me, pray!"
* And I said, "How ugly to see!"

Then a truly angelic smile
Shone on your fair face,
That methought I espied
The sky open in embrace.

And then I took you aside
By a rosebush in bloom,
Slowly I let my head hide
Into your snow-white arms.

Every kiss you gave me,
Dear soul, with sweetness,
Made a new rose appear
On the bush, with swiftness.

They were aborning all night,
Till the early light of dawn
Which found us looking pale,
With faces tired and drawn.

My soul, this was my vision.
It is now up to you
To remember me and make
This sweet dream come true!

K. Mitsakis, *Modern Greek Music and Poetry: An Anthology.*
(Athens: Grigoris, 1979), pp. 146-9.

* Τότε ἄκουσα τό χείλι
* Τό δικό σου νά μοῦ πῆ:
* Πῶς σοῦ φαίνονται; Καί σοῦπα:
* Εἶναι ἄσχημες πολύ.

Ἐσύ ἔκαμες ἐτότες
Γέλιο τόσο ἀγγελικό,
Πού μοῦ φάνηκε πώς εἶδα
Ἀνοιχτό τόν οὐρανό.

Καί παράμερα σ᾽ ἐπῆρα
Εἰσέ μία τρανταφυλλιά
Κι᾽ ἔπεσά σου ἀγάλι ἀγάλι
Στήν ὁλόλευκη ἀγκαλιά.

Κάθε φίλημα, ψυχή μου,
Ὁπού μ᾽ ὄδινες γλυκά,
Ἐξεφύτρωνε ἄλλο ρόδο
Ἀπό τήν τρανταφυλλιά.

Ὅλη νύχτα ἐξεφυτρῶσαν,
Ὡς ὁποῦλαμψεν ἡ αὐγή,
Πού μᾶς ηὖρε καί τούς δυό μας
Μέ τήν ὄψη μας χλωμή.

Τοῦτο εἶν᾽ τ᾽ ὄνειρο, ψυχή μου·
Τώρα στέκεται εἰς ἐσέ
Νά τό κάμης ν᾽ ἀληθέψη
Καί νά θυμηθῆς γιά μέ.

39

from *Hymn to Liberty*
the National Anthem of Greece

1.

I know you by the sharp blade
of your terrifying sword,
I know you by the form you made
taking the earth as victor lord.

2.

Sprung from Grecian bones scattered
hallowed on every vale,
with your old valor unshattered,
Liberty, hail to you, hail!

15.

Yes, but your sons, your offspring
now fight with all their breath,
and unceasingly are seeking
either victory or death.

155.

"Images of the Most High
can't you hear this cry of pain?
Centuries have passed it by
but its echo does remain.

157.

What then? Will you allow us
to struggle and become freed?
Or will you disavow us
due to politicians' need?

158.

If this is then your decision
here, before you stands the Cross!
Crush it, Monarchs, to oblivion,
crush it, help to wreak our loss."

Hellenic Chronicle (20 March 1975), 3.

Ὕμνος εἰς τήν Ἐλευθερία

1.
Σέ γνωρίζω ἀπό τήν κόψη
Τοῦ σπαθιοῦ τήν τρομερή,
Σέ γνωρίζω ἀπό τήν ὄψη
Πού μέ βία μετράει τή γῆ.

2.
Ἀπ᾿ τά κόκαλα βγαλμένη
Τῶν Ἑλλήνων τά ἱερά,
Καί σάν πρῶτα ἀνδρειωμένη,
Χαῖρε, ὦ χαῖρε, Ἐλευθεριά!

15
Ναί· ἀλλά τώρα ἀντιπαλεύει
Κάθε τέκνο σου μέ ὁρμή,
Πού ἀκατάπαυστα γυρεύει
Ἤ τή νίκη ἤ τή θανή.

155
Δέν ἀκοῦτε, ἐσεῖς εἰκόνες
Τοῦ Θεοῦ, τέτοια φωνή;
Τώρα ἐπέρασαν αἰῶνες
Καί δέν ἔπαυσε στιγμή.

157
Τί θά κάμετε; θ᾿ ἀφῆστε
Νά ἀποκτήσωμεν ἐμεῖς
Λευθερίαν, ἤ θά τήν λύστε
Ἐξ αἰτίας Πολιτικῆς;

158
Τοῦτο ἀνίσως μελετᾶτε,
Ἰδού, ἐμπρός σας τόν Σταυρό·
Βασιλεῖς! ἐλᾶτε, ἐλᾶτε,
Καί κτυπήσετε κι᾿ ἐδῶ.

Epigram to Psara

On Psara's blackened, charred stone
Glory silently walks all alone
meditating her sons' noble deeds,
and wears a wreath on her hair
made of such few scattered weeds
on the desolate earth left to spare.

Hellenic Chronicle, (20 March, 1975), 3.

Η Καταστροφή τῶν Ψαρῶν

Στῶν Ψαρῶν τήν ὁλόμαυρη ράχη
Περπατώντας ἡ Δόξα μονάχη
Μελετᾶ τά λαμπρά παλληκάρια
Καί στήν κόμη στεφάνι φορεῖ
Γεναμένο ἀπό λίγα χορτάρια
Πού εἶχαν μείνει στήν ἔρημη γῆ.

From *Lyrical Poem on the Death of Lord Byron*

1. Liberty, cease for a moment
    Striking hard with your sword;
    Now approach here to lament
    By the body of this noble lord;

6. Valiant Byron was raised
    Amid clanging arms in use;
    While still young he was graced
    By the one melodic Muse.

12. "Sing, oh Byron," she cried,
    "All the beauties you can see!"
    And readily he replied,
    Having heard her honest plea.

13. In response he sang sweetly
    In his most melodious rime,
    Human passions touching deeply
    With his poems most sublime.

45. In Greece now people rejoice,
    For the Man she was seeking
    Is seen coming, and his voice
    Like a war drum is beating.

81. Byron to them did declare:
    "Quit Erinys, side with Greece!
    What are you doing? Where?
    Let among you all be peace!"

106. Alas! Why Byron returning
    Found these brave men crestfallen?
    Weeping they were and yearning:
    Their most glorious man had fallen.

Εἰς τό θάνατο τοῦ Λόρδ Μπάϋρον-Ποίημα Λυρικό

1. Λευθεριά γιά λίγο πᾶψε
   νά κτυπᾶς μέ τό σπαθί
   Τώρα σίμωσε καί κλᾶψε
   εἰς τοῦ Μπάϋρον τό κορμί

6. ᾽Αναθράφηκε ὁ γενναῖος
   Στῶν ἀρμάτων τήν κλαγγή·
   Τοῦτον ἔμπνευσε, ὄντας νέος,
   Μιά θεά μελωδική.

12. Ψάλλε, Μπάϋρον, τοῦ λαλοῦσε,
    ῞Οσες βλέπεις ὀμορφιές·
    Καί ᾽κειός, πού ἐκρυφαγροικοῦσε
    ᾽Ανταπόκριση μ᾽ αὐτές,

13. Βάνεται, τές τραγουδάει
    Μ᾽ ἕνα χεῖλο ἀρμονικό,
    Καί τά πάθη ἔτσι σοῦ ᾽γγιάει,
    Πού τραγούδι πλέον ᾽ψηλό.

45. Στήν ῾Ελλάδα χαροκόπι·
    Γιατί ᾽Εκεῖνον, πού ζητεῖ,
    Βλέπει νἄρχεται, καί οἱ τόποι
    Πού ἡ σκλαβιά καταπατεῖ,

81. Καί τούς φώναξε: «Φευγᾶτε
    Τσ᾽ ᾽Ερινύας τήν τρικυμιά·
    ῏Ω! τί κάνετε; Ποῦ πᾶτε;
    Γιά φερθῆτε εἰρηνικά!»

106. Γιατί, ἀλίμονο! γυρίζοντας
     Τσ᾽ ηὗρε ὁ Μπάϋρον σκυθρωπούς;
     ᾽Εγυρεύανε δακρύζοντας
     Τόν πλέον ἔνδοξο ἀπ᾽ αὐτούς.

45

115. Tell me, valiant, what direction
Do your daring thoughts crave,
While for long, with discretion,
Linger by Markos's grave?

131. "God, make him our home to find
And live with my dearest mother;
Come quickly father, be kind,
England awaits none other."

134. Alas! Who will ever give us
A little early consolation?
Byron won't remain among us,
Nor his ashes for protection.

165. Byron full of respect paces
And looks restlessly with care,
At the wounds and at the faces,
Thus addressing those there:

166. "Discord in Greece again reigns,
If the two of them you can sever,
BY THE WORLD THAT ALL CONTAINS,
Your name shall live forever!"

115. Πές μου, 'Ανδρεῖε, τί μελετοῦνε
      Οἱ γενναῖοι σου στοχασμοί,
      Πού πολληώρα ἀργοποροῦνε
      Εἰς τοῦ Μάρκου τήν ταφή;

131. «Κάμε 'Εσύ μέ τήν μητέρα
      Τή γλυκειά μου νά ἐνωθῆ
      "Ελα γλήγορα, πατέρα,
      "Ολη ἡ 'Αγγλία σέ καρτερεῖ.»

134. Ποιός ἀλίμονον! μᾶς δίνει
      Μιάν ἀρχή παρηγοριᾶς;
      'Απ' αὐτόν δέ θέ νά μείνη
      Μήτε ἡ στάχτη του μέ μᾶς·

165. 'Κειός σεβάσμια προχωρῶντας
      Καί μέ ἀνήσυχες ματιές,
      Τά προσώπατα κοιτῶντας,
      Καί κοιτῶντας τίς πληγές:

166. «'Η Διχόνοια κατατρέχει
      Τήν 'Ελλάδα ἄν νικηθῆ,
      ΜΑ ΤΟΝ ΚΟΣΜΟ ΠΟΥ ΜΑΣ ΕΧΕΙ,
      Τ' ὄνομά σας ξαναζῆ.»

Ode to Botsaris

Glory stands to the right
of the man who moves with pain
through Fame's roughest terrain;
Envy stands by his left side,
tight-lipped, bitter-eyed.

But when his destiny ordains
the worldly ways he disdains;
Glory then sits all alone
on the glowing tombstone,
and Envy walks elsewhere.

On the humble hero's tombstone
Glory sits amid glowing splendor;
the eyes that shone with fervor,
when he fought, are now closed forever.
Boys, approach and listen together!

Wordmongers, keep away from here!
Lest my words hurt your fine ear;
run into the serried graves
chanting wildly as one who raves.
Boys, approach and listen together!

The body that Priam had rescued
with many a gift and lament,
was brought back that moment
when rosy dawn's mild light
on the face of the earth does alight.

All of them got out together
from sad Troy's each human fold,
women, children, young men and old,
sobbing, they wanted the body to see
that had lost its soul for their sake.

Εἰς Μάρκο Μπότσαρη

Ἡ Δόξα δεξιά συντροφεύει
Τόν ἄντρα πού τρέχει μέ κόπους
Τῆς Φήμης τούς δύσβατους τόπους,
Καί ὁ Φθόνος τοῦ στέκει ζερβά,
Μέ μάτια, μέ χείλη πικρά·

Ἀλλ' ὅποτε ἡ μοίρα του γράψη,
Τόν δρόμον τοῦ κόσμου νά πάψη,
Ἡ Δόξα καθίζει μονάχη
Στήν πλάκα τοῦ τάφου λαμπρή,
Καί ὁ Φθόνος ἀλλοῦ περπατεῖ.

Στήν πλάκα τοῦ Μάρκου καθίζει
Ἡ Δόξα λαμπράδες γιομάτη·
Κλεισμένο γιά πάντα τό μάτι,
Ὁποὖχε πολέμου φωτιά·—
Ἐλᾶτε ν' ἀκοῦστε, παιδιά!

Σοφοί λεξιθῆρες, μακρία—
Μή λάχη σᾶς βλάψω τ' αὐτία·
Τρεχᾶτε στά μνήματα μέσα
Καί ψάλτε μέ λόγια τρελά·—
Ἐλᾶτε ν' ἀκοῦστε, παιδιά!

Τό λείψανο ποὖχε γλυτώσει
Ὁ Πρίαμος μέ θρήνους, μέ δῶρα,
Ἐγύριζε ὀπίσω τήν ὥρα
Πού πέφτει στήν ὄψη τῆς γῆς
Τό φῶς τό γλυκό τῆς αὐγῆς.

Ἐβγῆκαν μαζί τῆς θλιμμένης
Τρωάδας ἀπ' ὅλα τά μέρη
Γυναῖκες, παιδάκια καί γέροι,
Θρηνώντας, νά ἰδοῦν τό κορμί
Πού χάνει γι' αὐτούς τήν ψυχή.

Every mouth shouted loud
over Markos' body in its shroud;
"He is gone, our Markos is gone!"
There was clamor of sadness and pain,
cries and sobs were heard on the plain.

. . . .

A similar echo will resound
on the world's last day and most dear,
all over the new atmosphere:
it will reach the tombs in each section
and will bring to the dead resurrection.

Greek World, (March-April, 1976), 42.

Κλεισμένο δέν ἔμεινε στόμα
'Απάνου στοῦ Μάρκου τό σῶμα·
'Απέθαν', ἀπέθαν' ὁ Μάρκος·
Μιά θλίψη, μία ἄκρα βοή,
Καί θρῆνος καί κλάψα πολλή.

. . . .

Παρόμοια ἠχώ θά λαλήση,
Τοῦ κόσμου τήν ὕστερη μέρα,
Παντοῦ στόν καινούριον ἀέρα·
Παρόμοια στούς τάφους θά ἐμβῆ,
Νά κάμη καθένας νά ἐβγῆ.

To Francesca Fraser

A minor prophet gazed once upon a pure maiden
And in his most secret thoughts jubilant he exclaimed:
"Even if for your feet, Beautiful Girl, even if for your face,
Lilies the stone sprouted forth, the sun a golden crown,
These gifts are unworthy of You and the wealth within You.
A beautiful moral world, the creation of angels" (I, 260).

M.B. Raizis, *Dionysios Solomos* (Boston: Twayne, 1972), p. 121.

Eurycome

"Ocean, when will I get to see the fair Eurycome?
A long time has passed and she has not come to me.
How often stooping on the rock anxiously I and pale
Mistook the foam of the sea for her white sail!
Bring her back, bring her at last!" So Thyrsis exclaims,
And takes water from the sea, kísses it, and complains;
And he doesn't know, the miserable, that he is kissing the wave
The same that has given her death as well as a grave.

C. Th. Dimaras, *A History of Modern Greek Literature* (Albany: S.U.N.Y. Press, 1972), p. 230.

Εἰς Φραγκίσκα Φραῖζερ

Μικρός προφήτης ἔριξε σέ Κορασιά τά μάτια
Καί στούς κρυφούς του λογισμούς χαρά γιομάτους εἶπε:
"Κι' ἄν γιά τά πόδια σου, Καλή, κι' ἄν γιά τήν κεφαλή σου,
κρίνους ὁ λίθος ἔβγανε, χρυσό στεφάν' ὁ ἥλιος
Δῶρο δέν ἔχουνε γιά Σέ καί γιά τό μέσα πλοῦτος.
῎Ομορφος κόσμος ἠθικός ἀγγελικά πλασμένος!"

῾Η Εὐρυκόμη

"Θάλασσα, πότε θέλ' ἰδῶ τήν ὄμορφη Εὐρυκόμη;
Πολύς καιρός ἐπέρασε καί δέν τήν εἶδα ἀκόμη.
Πόσες φορές κοιτάζοντας ἀπό τό βράχο γέρνω
Καί τόν ἀφρό τῆς θάλασσας γιά τά πανιά της παίρνω!
Φέρ' τηνε, τέλος, φέρ' τηνε." Αὐτά ὁ Θύρσης λέει,
Καί παίρνει ἀπό τή θάλασσα καί τή φιλεῖ καί κλαίει·
Καί δέν ἠξέρει ὁ δύστυχος ὁπού φιλεῖ τό κύμα
᾽Εκεῖνο, πού τῆς ἔδωσε καί θάνατο καί μνῆμα.

To the Death of his Niece

Thrice she glanced at the high mirror
That reflected her graceful nuptial gown
That her image wore, and the crown;
The maiden solemn and speechless
Looked around her thrice, not less.

C. Th. Dimaras, *A History of Modern Greek Literature* (Albany: S.U.N.Y. Press, 1972), p. 230.

from *Lambros*

Maria comes forth seeking the solace
Of coolness for her hope-forsaken breast;
The night is sweet, and the full-moon's face
Has not emerged, any star's glow to contest;
Multitudes, myriads, they glimmer in all their grace
Some solitarily, some others abreast;
They too are celebrating the Resurrection
That is mirrored on the calm sea's reflection. (I, 187)

Downward he cast his face, pale as sulphur,
And in a low voice these words he hurled:
"The Saints are dumb and lifeless, no murmur
Comes from the tombs; cried I till the midnight wild.
Man (despite destiny's will and design), a cur,
Is the only God of himself; he always excelled
In time of utter wretchedness. Despair,
Hide in my soul and rest for ever there." (I, 188)

M.B. Raizis, *Dionysios Solomos* (Boston: Twayne, 1972), p. 105.

Εἰς τό Θάνατο τῆς Ἀνεψιᾶς του

Στόν καθρέφτη π' ἀκέριαν ἐδέχτη
Τή γλυκιά τῆς παρθένας εἰκόνα
Μέ τοῦ γάμου στολές καί κορόνα
Ρίχνει τρεῖς ἡ παρθένα ματιές
Τρεῖς κινώντας τριγύρου φορές.

ἀπό τό Λάμπρο

Καί προβαίνει ἡ Μαρία λίγη νά πάρη
Δροσιά στά σωθικά τά μαραμένα·
Εἶναι νύκτα γλυκιά, καί τό φεγγάρι
Δέ βγαίνει νά σκεπάση ἄστρο κανένα·
Περίσσια, μύρια, σ' ὅλη τους τή χάρη,
Λάμπουν ἄλλα μονάχα, ἄλλα δεμένα·
Κάνουν καί κεῖνα Ἀνάσταση πού πέφτει
Τοῦ ὁλόστρωτου πελάου μές στόν καθρέφτη.

Καί τό πρόσωπο γέρνει ὡσάν τό θειάφι
Καί χαμηλά τοῦτα τά λόγια ρίχτει·
"Κουφοί, ἀκίνητ' οἱ Ἅγιοι, καθώς καί οἱ τάφοι·
Εἶπα κι' ἔκραξα ὥς τ' ἄγριο μεσονύχτι.
Ἄντρας (κι' ἡ μοίρα ὅ,τι κι' ἄ θέλη ἄς γράφη)
Τοῦ ἑαυτοῦ του εἶναι Θεός, καί δείχτει
Στήν ἄκρα δυστυχία· μές στήν ψυχή μου
Κάθου κρυμμένη, ἀπελπισιά, καί κοίμου."

The Free Besieged
Draft III

1

Oh you Mother magnanimous in suffering and glory,
Even if your children always live in a mystery hidden,
In meditation and in dream, what has graced my eyes,
My very eyes to see you in this deserted forest,
Which quite suddenly has wreathed your deathless feet
(Look) with Easter Palms, the greenery of Palm Sunday!
My ears missed your holy step, my eyes missed your figure,
Serene you are like the sky enriched by all its beauties,
That show in many places, in others they are hidden;
But, Goddess, may I hear at last the sound of your voice,
At once to make it a gift to the Hellenic nation?
On its black rocks and dried grass glory dwells forever.

2

Deeds, words, and deep thoughts—motionless, I stare—
Myriads of blossoms, colorful, cover the grassy carpet,
White, red, blue invite bees of a golden hue.
Away, one lives among friends, but here, in death's presence.
Often upon the break of dawn and in the midst of day,
When the waters turned dark, and the stars grew in numbers,
Beaches, rocks, and the open sea suddenly leap up and quiver.
Arabic chargers, English guns, Turkish shots, French minds!
A great ocean makes war and strikes the tiny cottage;
* Alas! In a while uncovered the few bosoms remain;
Thunder are you deathless, have you never known rest?
That's what a sailor from abroad says bending over the prow,
All round in fear the islands, they all weep and pray,
And the cross-shaped domed temple and the most modest
    shrine
Amid incense and lit candles listen to their pain.
Hatred, though, made heard its odious voice also:
"Fisherwoman, take your hook and go cast elsewhere".

56

Ἐλεύθεροι Πολιορκημένοι
Σχεδίασμα Γ΄

1

Μητέρα, μεγαλόψυχη στόν πόνο καί στή δόξα,
Κι᾽ ἄν στό κρυφό μυστήριο ζοῦν πάντα τά παιδιά σου
Μέ λογισμό καί μ᾽ ὄνειρο, τί χάρ᾽ ἔχουν τά μάτια,
Τά μάτια τοῦτα, νά σ᾽ ἰδοῦν μές στό πανέρμο δάσος,
Πού ξάφνου σοῦ τριγύρισε τ᾽ ἀθάνατα ποδάρια
(Κοίτα) μέ φύλλα τῆς Λαμπρῆς, μέ φύλλα τοῦ Βαϊῶνε!
Τό θεϊκό σου πάτημα δέν ἄκουσα, δέν εἶδα,
Ἀτάραχη σάν οὐρανός μ᾽ ὅλα τά κάλλη πὄχει,
Πού μέρη τόσα φαίνονται καί μέρη ᾽ναι κρυμμένα·
Ἀλλά, Θεά, δέν ἠμπορῶ ν᾽ ἀκούσω τή φωνή σου,
Κι᾽ εὐθύς ἐγώ τ᾽ Ἑλληνικοῦ κόσμου νά τή χαρίσω;
Δόξα ᾽χ᾽ ἡ μαύρη πέτρα σου καί τό ξερό χορτάρι.

2

Ἔργα καί λόγια, στοχασμοί,—στέκομαι καί κοιτάζω—
Λούλουδα μύρια πούλουδα, πού κρύβουν τό χορτάρι,
Κι᾽ ἄσπρα, γαλάζια, κόκκινα, καλοῦν χρυσό μελίσσι.
Ἐκεῖθε μέ τούς ἀδελφούς, ἐδῶθε μέ τό χάρο.—
Μές στά χαράματα συχνά, καί μές στά μεσημέρια,
Καί σά θολώσουν τά νερά, καί τ᾽ ἄστρα σά πληθύνουν,
Ξάφνου σκιρτοῦν οἱ ἀκρογιαλιές, τά πέλαγα κι᾽ οἱ βράχοι.
«Ἀραπιᾶς ἄτι, Γάλλου νοῦς, βόλι Τουρκιᾶς, τόπ᾽ Ἄγγλου!
Πέλαγο μέγα πολεμᾶ, βαρεῖ τό καλυβάκι·
Κι᾽ ἀλιά! σέ λίγο ξέσκεπα τά λίγα στήθη μένουν·
Ἀθάνατη ᾽σαι, πού ποτέ, βροντή, δέν ἡσυχάζεις;»
Στήν πλώρη, πού σκιρτᾶ, γυρτός, τοῦτά ᾽π᾽ ὁ ξένος ναύτης.
Δειλιάζουν γύρου τά νησιά, παρακαλοῦν καί κλαῖνε,
Καί μέ λιβάνια δέχεται καί φῶτα τόν καημό τους
Ὁ σταυροθόλωτος ναός καί τό φτωχό ξωκλήσι.
Τό μίσος ὅμως ἔβγαλε καί κεῖνο τή φωνή του:
«Ψαρού, τ᾽ ἀγκίστρι, π᾽ ἄφισες, ἀλλοῦ νά ρίξης ἄμε».

57

2a

Often at the break of dawn, and in the midst of day,
When the waters turn dark, and the stars grow in numbers,
Beaches, rocks, and the open sea suddenly leap up and quiver.
An old man, who had stuck his life to the fish-hook,
Cast it away, missed his mark, and pacing he cried:
"Arabic chargers, English guns, Turkish shots, French minds!
Alas, a great ocean strikes hard the tiny cottage;
* In a little while uncovered the few bosoms remain;
* Thunder are you deathless, have you never known rest?
* Oh desolation I can see, come, let us weep together".

3

The war has not exhausted them, it has become their life,
. . . . cannot prevent
The girls from singing songs, the boys from playing games.

4

Out of clouds ever black, out of the pitch of darkness,
. . . .
But sunlike then, invisible ether of a world in symbol
The flagpole appears, the brave warriors underneath it,
And up there, on its highest end, the banner in full glory,
That speaks and murmurs and its Cross waves in the air
In all the space around it, the brave wind of valor,
The sky looked on proudly and all the earth applauded;
And every voice stirring then toward the light echoed,
Most noble flowers of love scattering all around;
* "Unconquered, rich, and beautiful, venerable too, and
holy!"

K. Mitsakis *Modern Greek Music and Poetry*. Athens: Grigoris
1979, 154-157.

Μές στά χαράματα συχνά, καί μές στά μεσημέρια,
Κι᾿ ὅταν θολώσουν τά νερά, κι᾿ ὅταν πληθύνουν τ᾿ ἄστρα,
Ξάφνου σκιρτοῦν οἱ ἀκρογιαλιές, τά πέλαγα κι᾿ οἱ βράχοι.
Γέρος μακριά, π᾿ ἀπίθωσε στ᾿ ἀγκίστρι τή ζωή του,
Τό πέταξε, τ᾿ ἀστόχησε καί περιτριγυρνώντας:
«᾿Αραπιᾶς ἄτι, Γάλλου νοῦς, βόλι Τουρκιᾶς, τόπ᾿ ῎Αγγλου!
Πέλαγο, μέγ᾿ ἀλίμονον! βαρεῖ τό καλυβάκι·
* Σέ λίγην ὥρα ξέσκεπα τά λίγη στήθη μένουν·
* ᾿Αθάνατή ᾿σαι, πού, βροντή, ποτέ δέν ἡσυχάζεις;
* Πανερημιά τῆς γνώρας μου, θέλω μ᾿ ἐμέ νά κλάψης».

3

Δέν τούς βαραίν᾿ ὁ πόλεμος, ἀλλ᾿ ἔγινε ἡ πνοή τους,
. . . . κι᾿ ἐμπόδισμα δέν εἶναι
Στές κορασιές νά τραγουδοῦν καί στά παιδιά νά παίζουν.

4

᾿Από τό μαῦρο σύγνεφο κι᾿ ἀπό τή μαύρη πίσσα,
. . . .
᾿Αλλ᾿ ἥλιος, ἀλλ᾿ ἀόρατος αἰθέρας κοσμοφόρος
῾Ο στύλος φανερώνεται, μέ κάτου μαζωμένα
Τά παλληκάρια τά καλά, μ᾿ ἀπάνου τή σημαία,
Πού μουρμουρίζει καί μιλεῖ καί τό Σταυρόν ἀπλώνει
Παντόγυρα στόν ὄμορφον ἀέρα τῆς ἀντρείας,
Κι᾿ ὁ οὐρανός καμάρωνε, κι᾿ ἡ γῆ χεροκροτοῦσε·
κάθε φωνή κινούμενη κατά τό φῶς μιλοῦσε,
Κι᾿ ἐσκόρπα τά τρισεύγενα λουλούδια τῆς ἀγάπης:
«῎Ομορφη, πλούσια, κι᾿ ἄπαρτη, καί σεβαστή, κι᾿ ἁγία!»

JOHN POLEMIS

Epigramme (to Byron)

Glory—that with innocent hands, with hands purified
and with an immaculate blade, a blade holy and clean
cut fresh branches of Delphic laurel tree and tied
them in haste making a wreath for ever green
to crown you in your last bed since you fell,
—death has crowned her as well.

Balkan Studies, **XX**, No. 2 (1979), 307.

ΙΩΑΝΝΗΣ ΠΟΛΕΜΗΣ

Ἐπίγραμμα (στόν Βύρωνα)

Τή Δόξα, πού μέ χέρια ἁγνά, χέρια καθάρια
καί μέ δρεπάνι ἀμόλυντο, ἱερό δρεπάνι,
ἔκοψε δάφνης δελφικῆς χλωρά κλωνάρια
κ' ἔπλεξε βιαστικά τό ἀμάραντο στεφάνι
γιά νά σέ στεφανώση στή στερνή σου κλίνη,
ὁ θάνατός σου τή στεφάνωσε κ' ἐκείνη.

GEORGE DROSINIS

The Death of the Swan

Where the black coot and the wild duck
find a wintering place upon the sunny land,
White Swan of the north, what did you seek to pluck
by the lagoon's decaying wateredge and sand?

The world-seducing Swan, by a lagoon Mermaid
had been seduced—Freedom she was called;
For her palace on earth the battery had made,
bedecked not like a bride but in a panoply bold.

The White Swan then tried an eagle's form to take,
eagle-like wings and talons stretching for her sake;
but his foolhardy attempt proved to be fatal . . .
And when, in mid spring, the waterfowl flew forth
returning to the far distant shore of the north,
an   escort they became to the Swan's funeral . . .

Balkan Studies, XX, No. 2 (1979), 305-6.

ΓΕΩΡΓΙΟΣ ΔΡΟΣΙΝΗΣ

Ὁ θάνατος τοῦ κύκνου

᾿Εκεῖ πού ἡ μαύρη φαλαρίδα κι ἡ ἄγρια πάπια
χειμαδιό βρίσκουν στήν προσηλιακή στεριά,
στῆς λιμνοθάλασσας τ᾿ ἀκρόνερα τά σάπια
τί ἦρθες ζητώντας, λευκέ Κύκνε, τοῦ βοριά;

Τόν Κύκνο κοσμοπλάνευτη πλάνεψε κάποια
τῆς λιμνοθάλασσας νεράϊδα, ἡ Λευτεριά·
Παλάτι στεριανό τοῦ κάστρου εἶχε τήν τάπια,
κι ἀντί στολίδια νύφης, ἄρματα βαριά.

᾿Αητός ὁ λευκός κύκνος θέλησε νά γίνει,
κι ἀητοῦ φτερά καί νύχια τάνυσε γιά κείνη·
μά ἦταν θανάσιμη ἡ παράτολμή του ὁρμή . . .
Καί τά μαγιάπριλα ὅταν γύριζαν καί πάλι
τά νεροπούλια πρός τό βοριανό ἀκρογιάλι,
συνοδιά γίνηκαν στοῦ Κύκνου τό κορμί . . .

JOHN GRYPARIS

Childe Harold

On the waves sliding the boat seemed unreal and spectral;
the orphan Moon cast barren light upon her lone way,
clad in black veils the mourners at the funeral
neither sighed, nor shed tears, nor a word did say.

Lo . . . the Bard, lying dead, is going homebound . . .
forehead uncovered, eyes open . . . as if he was drinking
the faint glow of the Moon . . . hearing the soft sound
of the stern's final harmony that was slowly sinking.

But who is groaning afar, in the ever distant shore?
the Nymph must be, the ailing Mermaid in her pain
asking an end to life and sorrow she can bear no more . . .

Meanwhile, the boat silently its secret port did gain,
while the waves timidly in constant undulation
its sides touched with warmth as if in lamentation . . .

Balkan Studies, XX, No. 2 (1979), 304.

ΙΩΑΝΝΗΣ ΓΡΥΠΑΡΗΣ

Τσάιλδ Χάρολδ

Σάν φάντασμα στά κύματα γλιστρᾶ ἡ βάρκα· ραίνει
μέ στεῖρο φῶς τό δρόμο της πεντάρφανη ἡ Σελήνη
καί τοῦ λειψάνου ἡ συνοδιά μαῦρες σκεπές ντυμένη,
βουβή, μήδ᾽ ἕνα στεναγμό, μήδ᾽ ἕνα δάκρυ χύνει.

Νά . . . ξαπλωμένος ὁ νεκρός τραγουδιστής πηγαίνει . . .
μέτωπο ξέσκεπο . . . ἀνοιχτά τά μάτια . . . σά νά πίνει
τοῦ φεγγαριοῦ τ᾽ ἀπόφεγγα . . . σά νά γροικάει πού βγαίνει
στερνή ἁρμονία ἀπ᾽ τή συρμή τῆς πρύμης πού ἀργοσβήνει.

Μά τί βογγάει στό ἀλαργινό, πού χάνεται ἀκρογιάλι;
θέ νάναι ἡ Νύφη, ἡ ἄρρωστη Νεράϊδα, πού σπαράζει
ζητώντας μέ τόν πόνο της καί τήν ψυχή νά βγάλει . . .

῾Ωστόσο ἡ βάρκα στό κρυφό τό ἀραξοβόλι ἀράζει,
ἐνῶ τά κύματα σκιαχτά μιά ἔρχονται μιά πᾶνε
καί στά πλευρά της σά ζεστό παράπονο χτυπᾶνε . . .

KOSTAS KARYOTAKIS

Byron

He became aware
That verse was to him
Sad fate's whim
And vanity's fair.

Splendour so great
Up the city's walls
And brave youth falls
By lagoon and gate!

Old age grows
Bold; valiant men
Will storm out strong.

And Byron knows
To live and pen
The divine song.

The Byron Society *Newsletter,* IV, No. 1 (1976), 17.

ΚΩΣΤΑΣ ΚΑΡΥΩΤΑΚΗΣ

Μπάϋρον

Ένοιωσεν ὅτι
τοῦ ἦσαν οἱ στίχοι
ἄχαρη τύχη
καί ματαιότη.

Μά ποιά λαμπρότη
ἐκεῖ στά τείχη
καί ποιά στά ρήχη
ἔνδοξη νιότη!

Γίνονται οἱ γέροι
γαῦροι· θά ὁρμήσει
ἀνδρῶν λουλούδι,

κι ὁ Μπάϋρον ξέρει
πῶς νά τό ζήσει
τό θεῖο τραγούδι.

MICHAEL D. STASINOPOULOS

The Knight of Chess

Alert, calm, and silent, lost in his thoughts, the Knight
onto back or white spaces readily jumps and waits.
While deep thoughts fix him onto squares, black or white,
the sad and speechless game's turns he sees and calculates.

A move, another move, a thought, another thought.
Round him wooden enemies and their devious goals.
What can he think of, devise, consider with care?
The narrow squares heavily have taxed his thought
and his life turned monotonous with a familiar air.

A move, another move; a thought—the same thought!
He counts and reckons silently the game's every move,
—but well he knows that destiny his life did ordain
to charge his wooden enemies and among them to fall,
onto black or white squares, bravely, beside his sovereign.

ΜΙΧΑΗΛ Δ. ΣΤΑΣΙΝΟΠΟΥΛΟΣ

Τό ἄλογο τοῦ σκακιοῦ

Προσεχτικό κι᾿ ἀσάλευτο, βουβό κι ἀφαιρεμένο
στό μαῦρο ἤ στ᾿ ἄσπρο, ὑπάκουο πηδάει καί περιμένει.
Στό μαῦρο ἤ στ᾿ ἄσπρο, ἀσάλευτο, βαθιά συλλογισμένο,
τό σκυθρωπό κι ἀμίλητο παιγνίδι λογαριάζει.

Μιά κίνηση, ἄλλη κίνηση, μιά σκέψη, κι ἄλλη σκέψη.
Τριγύρω οἱ ξύλινοι του ἐχθροί κι οἱ ἐπίβουλοι σκοποί τους.
Τί νά σκεφτεῖ, νά σοφιστεῖ καί τί νά λογαριάσει;
Μές στά στενά τετράγωνα ἐσώθηκεν ἡ σκέψη
κι᾿ ἔγινε πιά μονότονη καί γνώριμη ἡ ζωή του.

Μιά κίνηση, ἄλλη κίνηση, μιά σκέψη—ἡ ἴδια σκέψη!
Τό σιωπηλό παιγνίδι του μετρᾶ καί λογαριάζει,
—μά ὅμως τό ξέρει πώς γραφτό σ᾿ ὅλη εἶναι τή ζωή του,
νά ὁρμᾶ μέσα στούς ξύλινους ἐχθρούς του, καί νά πέφτει,
στό μαῦρο ἤ στ᾿ ἄσπρο, ἡρωϊκά, κοντά στό βασιλιά του.

NIKOS KAZANTZAKIS

from *Odysseus,* A Drama

And you abandon your fortune to the suitors
And do not dare utter a word in protest!
They're after your mother like dogs in heat,
And you stare at the sea, and expect the
Hands of an old man to come and save you!
Do you want to be like him? Then buckle
His sword and go to the palace to kill!
Ah, if he were to put his foot here again
Your island would shake with terror,
And the suitors would keep quiet like deer
That have scented a lion's breath;
And they would pay with black blood
For their ignoble and most indecent feasts!

. . . . . .

Greetings to you, my Lords; where are you going?
The doors are barred, and in my wide courts,
O bridegrooms, the wedding's about to begin!
Eh you woman, go crouch in the corner,
Take care—an arrow may wound you,
Lady, in the tumult of the massacre!—
I'm Odysseus, and my faithful bow
Has recognized me, it dances in my hand
And the string sings like a swallow full of joy!
And in my tight grip death shines calm,
Like a thunderbolt in a just man's hand!

Fairleigh Dickinson University *The Literary Review,* XVI, No. 3 (Spring 1973), 352.

ΝΙΚΟΣ ΚΑΖΑΝΤΖΑΚΗΣ

άπό τό δράμα Όδυσσέας

Μά έσύ τό βιός σου άφήνεις στούς μνηστῆρες
καί δέν τολμᾶς κεφάλι νά σηκώσεις!
Τή μάνα σου τήν τρογυρνοῦν σά σκύλοι,
καί σύ τηρᾶς τή θάλασσα, καί χέρια
γεροντικά προσμένεις νά σέ σώσουν!
Θές νά τοῦ μοιάσεις; Ζῶσε τό σπαθί του
καί τράβα στό παλάτι νά σκοτώσεις!
Ἔ, νά πατοῦσε πάλι ἐδῶ τό πόδι του,
θά σειόταν τό νησί σας ἀπ' τόν τρόμο
κι ὡς λάφια θά λουφάζαν οἱ μνηστῆρες,
πού ὀσμίστηκαν τοῦ λιονταριοῦ τό χνῶτο·
καί θά πλερώναν μ' αἷμα μαῦρο τό ἄνομο
πολλά ξεδιάντροπο τους φαγοπότι!

. . . . . .

Καλῶς σᾶς βρῆκα, ἀρχόντοι μου· ποῦ πᾶτε;
Οἱ θύρες μανταλώθηκαν, κι ἀρχίζει,
γαμπροί, μές στίς φαρδιές αὐλές μου ὁ γάμος!
Ἔ σύ γυναίκα, στή γωνιά στριμώξου,
στό ἄναστα τῆς σφαγῆς μπορεῖ ἡ σαΐτα—
ἔχε τό νοῦ, κυρά—νά σέ λαβώσει!
Εἶμαι ὁ Δυσσέας, καί τό πιστό δοξάρι
μέ γνώρισε, στά χέρια μου χορεύει
κι ὅλο χαρά ἡ νευρά χελιδωνίζει!
Καί στίς βαριές μου φοῦχτες λάμπει ὁ θάνατος
γαλήνια, ὡς κεραυνός σέ δίκαιο χέρι!

Hymn from verse drama *Christ*

Virgin Mother, on whose untouched body the seed has fallen
like spirit and the Logos has become flesh feeding
on your ever virginal womb, like an infant!
My Lady Submission, you too accept the pain,
like the Cross, and bow your head
with patience, toward the earth, smiling,
my Lady, so that the world won't drown in your tears!
You are the Ark that shines on the abyss
like an egg and sails on God's dark seas,
guarding inside you the seeds of all!
You tread on the green crescent and,
holding all our hopes in your hands,
ascend to the untamed sky loaded and
faintly smiling, stand by your son.
You are the blooming branch on the abyss
of its strength; you are the meek thought
in the flaming furnace of its wrath.
You have planted the soft, tender tree of Goodness
in between the tree of Life and that of Knowledge
in God's garden. And it grows tall, watered by your tears,
sprouts branches, surpasses the other trees, blooms,
bears fruit like the good olive tree and shines.
And the Omnipotent rests in its shade.
And when the Second, the horrible, Coming arrives,
and the Archangels will ruthlessly separate
the goats from the sheep, you will stoop
to your son imploringly to intercede, Merciful Lady!
And at once his untamed mind will soften
and the columns will disperse, and the righteous
will embrace the sinners and be embraced, and pure virgins
will do so with women who had loved much on earth.
You defeat justice, You, with love!
And all of us together will start to dance, and you

ἀπό τό δρᾶμα Χριστός

Παρθένα Μανυ, που σάν πνέμα ἐπιάστη ὁ σπόρος
στό ἀφίλητο κορμί, κι ὁ Λόγος ἐσαρκώθη
τό ἀμόλευτο τρυγώντας σπλάχνο σου σά βρέφος!
Ὦ Δέσποινά μου Ὑποταγή, τόν πόνο δέξου τον
καί σύ, σάν τό σταυρό, καί γεῖρε τό κεφάλι
μέ ὑπομονή, κατά τή γῆς χαμογελώντας—
νά μήν πνιγεῖ, Κυρά, στά κλάματά σου ὁ κόσμος!
Ἐσύ 'σαι ἡ κιβωτός, πού σάν αὐγό στήν ἄβυσσο
λάμπεις καί στοῦ Θεοῦ τή σκοτεινιά ἀρμενίζεις,
βαθιά τά σπέρματα ὅλα μέσα σου φρουρώντας.
Τό πράσινο δρεπανωτό πατᾶς φεγγάρι,
κι ὅλες στά χέρια σου κρατώντας τίς ἐλπίδες μας
στόν ἄγριον οὐρανό κατάφορτη ἀνεβαίνεις·
κι ἀχνογελώντας στέκεσαι δεξιά στό γιό σου.
Ἐσύ 'σαι τό ἀνθισμένο τό κλαρί στήν ἄβυσσο
τῆς δύναμής του ἐσύ 'σαι ὁ στοχασμός ὁ πράος
μές στό φλεγόμενο καμίνι τῆς ὀργῆς του.
Ἀναμεσός στῆς Ζωῆς τό δένδρο καί τῆς Γνώσης,
στόν κῆπο τοῦ Θεοῦ σύ φύτεψες, Κυρά μου,
τό ἀφράτο, τρυφερό τῆς Καλοσύνης δένδρο·
κι ὡς πότιζες το μέ τό κλάμα, ἐπῆρε μπόι,
πετάει κλαριά, σκεπάζει τ' ἄλλα δέντρα, ἀνθίζει,
ρίχνει καρπό, σάν τήν καλήν ἐλιά, καί φέγγει—
κι ὁ Παντοδύναμος στόν ἴσκιο του ἀναπαύεται.
Κι ἡ Δεύτερη φριχτή σάν ἔρθει Παρουσία
κι οἱ ἀρχάγγελοι ἄσπλαχνα τά ρίφια θά χωρίζουν
ἀπό τ' ἀρνιά, θά σκύψεις τότε ἐσύ στό γιό σου,
παρακλητά, νά μεσιτέψεις, Ἐλεούσα!
Τ' ἀδάμαστα μεμιᾶς θά τοῦ μερώσουν φρένα
κι οἱ τάξεις θά χαλάσουν οἱ διπλές, καί δίκαιοι
θ' ἀγκαλιαστοῦν μέ ἁμαρτωλούς, κι ἁγνές παρθένες
μέ τίς γυναῖκες πού πολύ στή γῆς ἀγάπησαν.
Νικᾶς τή Δικαιοσύνη Ἐσύ μέ τήν ἀγάπη·
κι ὅλοι μαζί θά σύρουμε χορό, καί θά 'σαι

Lady will stand at the end of the line dancing in the unsetting sun of God joyful and very humble, like the heart of man.

Hellenism, vol. III, No 4 (April, 1970), 11. And, Seton Hall University, *Spirit,* XXXVII (Fall, 1970), 16-17.

ANDREAS EMBIRIKOS

The Verb To Perceive From Afar

This clear day with the cloud sailing in the air
Is a blue voyage of an all-white frigate
Leaning against the bulwarks I look out
And see the prey of my thinking
Dolphins emerging and submerging in the waves
Plains beaches and mountains
And a blond maiden standing by my side
In whose serene eyes I see
Her whole future and my present.

στόν κάβο τοῦ χοροῦ, Κυρά καί θά χορεύεις
στόν ἀβασίλευτο ἥλιο τοῦ Θεοῦ χαρούμενη
καί ταπεινή πολύ, σάν τήν καρδιά τοῦ ἀνθρώπου!

ΑΝΔΡΕΑΣ ΕΜΠΕΙΡΙΚΟΣ

Τό ρῆμα ἀγναντεύω

Τούτη ἡ αἰθρία μέ τό σύννεφο πού πλέχει στόν ἀέρα
Εἶναι γαλάζιος πλοῦς μιᾶς κάτασπρης φρεγάδας
Ἱστάμενος ἀκουμπιστός στήν κουπαστή κοιτάζω
Καί βλέπω τά θηράματα τῶν λογισμῶν μου
Δελφίνια πού ἀναδύονται κι᾿ εἰσδύουν μές τό κύμα
Πεδιάδες ἀκρογιάλια καί βουνά
Καί μιά ξανθή νεάνιδα πού στέκει στό πλευρό μου
Μές στῆς ὁποίας τά γαλήνια μάτια βλέπω
Τό μέλλον της ὁλόκληρο καί τό παρόν μου.

NIKOS ENGONOPOULOS

Vulture and Guard

hommage à apolLinaire

Mykonos	[=an island]	
Mykenai	[=Mycenae of Agamemnon]	Translator's note
myketes	[=fungi, in Greek]	
three		
words		
but		
only	like lime	
two	like a woman's	
wings	palm	
	shining	
	in	
	the night	and perhaps
	like a carnivorous	— even —
	violin	like the glass
		drills
		within the
		delicate
		brains
		of
		poets

(Engonopoulos is a surrealist painter as well).

ΝΙΚΟΣ ΕΓΓΟΝΟΠΟΥΛΟΣ

Γύψ καί φρουρά

hommage à apolLinaire

Μύκονος
Μυκῆναι
μύκητες
τρεῖς
λέξεις
ὅμως
μόνο   σάν ἀσβέστης
δύο   σάν γυναίκα
φτερά   παλάμη
          πού λάμπει
          μέσα   κι' ἴσως
          στή νύχτα —ἀκόμη—
          σά σαρκοβόρο ὡσάν τά γυάλινα
          βιολί   τρυπάνια
                    μέσα στούς
                    λεπτούς
                    ἐγκεφάλους
                    τῶν
                    ποιητῶν

MARKOS AVYERIS

I Proclaim Good News

I come from the wind
and march with the wind
My whole soul rejoices and goes
into the violent wind.

I am the Great Catalyst,
breath of Zeus, lord of the heights.

He smoothens the sharp edges of the rocks
and demolishes the dynasties of old
uplifting the great roads
and scattering the clouds
in the heavenly seas.

My soul rejoices in this storm
as a fountain dances in the sun.
There have I stored all my hopes
and my capital.

I hear the cry from tomorrow
that carries away the present,
fells the old trees
and sweeps away the other world's leaves.

It will cleanse the fumes
and will recycle the marshes
for the big rivers to flow free.

The time of the sun has now come
and it will descend and the prairies
will bloom and the mountains will turn green.

ΜΑΡΚΟΣ ΑΥΓΕΡΗΣ

Εὐαγγελίζομαι

Ἔρχομαι ἀπό τόν ἄνεμο
καί πορεύομαι μέ τόν ἄνεμο
Ὅλη ἡ ψυχή μου χαίρεται καί πάει
μέσα στό σφοδρόν ἄνεμο.

Εἶναι ὁ Μέγας Κατεβάτης,
πνοή τοῦ Δία τοῦ ἄρχοντα τῶν ὑψωμάτων.

Λειαίνει αὐτός τίς τραχειές ἐξοχές τῶν βράχων
καί γκρεμίζει τίς παλιές δυναστεῖες
ξεσηκώνοντας τούς μεγάλους δρόμους
καί σκορπώντας τά σύννεφα
στίς οὐράνιες θάλασσες.

Μέσα σ' αὐτή τή θύελλα χαίρεται ἡ ψυχή μου
ὅπως χορεύει ὁ πίδακας στόν ἥλιο.
Ἐκεῖ ἔχω ἀποθέσει ὅλες μου τίς ἐλπίδες
καί τά κεφάλαιά μου.

Ἀκούω τήν κραυγή ἀπό τό αὔριο
πού συνεπαίρνει τό σήμερα,
ρίχνει τά γέρικα δέντρα
καί σαρώνει τά φύλλα τοῦ ἄλλου κόσμου.

Θά καθαρίσει τίς ἀναθυμιάσεις
καί θ' ἀνακυκλίσει τά τέλματα
γιά νά τρέξουν ἐλεύθερα τά μεγάλα ποτάμια.

Εἶναι τώρα τοῦ ἥλιου ὁ καιρός
πού θά κατέβει καί θ' ἀνθίσουν οἱ πεδιάδες
καί θά πρασινίσουν τά βουνά.

I proclaim the wind and preach
the wind,
the drunken wind from the east
that brings the new sun.

It is the budding-wind
that makes the forests bloom.

I hear the wind
that comes from the peaks
and the valleys and the seas.

I preach the universal wind
of regeneration I announce
the wind that rekindles the flames,
within which the bird of fire sings.

I preach the wind of the new GENESIS.

Journal of the Hellenic American Society I, No. 3 (1974), 12-3.

Τόν ἄνεμο εὐαγγελίζομαι καί κηρύχνω
τόν ἄνεμο,
τό μεθυσμένον ἄνεμο τῆς ἀνατολῆς
πού φέρνει τόν καινούργιον ἥλιο.

Εἶναι ὁ φουσκοδέντρης
πού κάνει ν' ἀνθίζουν οἱ δρυμῶνες.

'Ακούω τόν ἄνεμο
πού ἔρχεται ἀπό τίς κορφές
ἀπό τούς κάμπους κι ἀπό τίς θάλασσες.

Κηρύχνω τόν καθολικόν ἄνεμο
τῆς παλιγγενεσίας ἀναγγέλλω
τόν ἄνεμο πού ξανάβει τίς πυρκαγιές,
πού μέσα τους τραγουδάει τό πουλί τῆς φωτιᾶς.

Κηρύχνω τόν ἄνεμο τῆς νέας ΓΕΝΕΣΕΩΣ.

NIKEPHOROS VRETTAKOS

An Almond Tree

An almond tree with you beside it.
But when did you two blossom?
Standing by the window
I look at you and weep.

My eyes can't bear such
mirth. God, give me
all the cisterns of heaven
and I'll fill them for you.

Peace

Love is in my heart like an almond tree branch
in a glass of water. The sun caresses it
and is filled with birds.
The best nightingale utters your name.

University of British Columbia
PRISM International, II, No. 1 (Summer, 1971), 62.

ΝΙΚΗΦΟΡΟΣ ΒΡΕΤΤΑΚΟΣ

Μιά μυγδαλιά

Μιά μυγδαλιά καί δίπλα της
ἐσύ. Μά πότε ἀνθήσατε;
Στέκομαι στό παράθυρο
καί σᾶς κυττῶ καί κλαίω.

Τόση χαρά δέν τήν μποροῦν
τά μάτια. Δός μου, Θεέ μου,
ὅλες τίς στέρνες τ' οὐρανοῦ
νά στίς γιομίσω.

Εἰρήνη

Εἶναι, ὅπως ἕνα κλωνάρι μυγδαλιᾶς σέ ποτήρι
στήν καρδιά μου ἡ ἀγάπη. Πέφτει πάνω της ὁ ἥλιος
καί γιομίζει πουλιά.
Τό καλύτερο ἀηδόνι λέει τ' ὄνομα σου.

The Purest Thing of Creation

I don't know how, but there isn't any darkness left at all.
The sun's poured itself inside me from a thousand wounds.
And this whiteness I'm covering you with
you won't find it even in the Alps, because this wind
whirls high up there too, and the snow becomes soiled.
Even on a white rose you find a speck of dust.
You'll find the perfect miracle only inside man:
white expanses that really glow
in the universe and stand out. The purest
thing of creation isn't then the twilight,
nor the sky reflected on the river, nor
the sun upon an apple-tree's blossoms. It is love.

An Epitaph

Bearing on his shoulders the Marathon trophy
the handsome dead lad is descending to Hades,
where the eternal Greeks are expecting him. But
he's bringing them only half of the message:

                                        WE HAVE
others after me are bringing you the WE HAVE WON.

I wasn't destined to come so early, I,
at the land of Plataea and Marathon,
was killed by the Persians.

Τό καθαρότερο πρᾶγμα τῆς δημιουργίας

Δέν ξέρω, μά δέν ἔμεινε καθόλου σκοτάδι.
Ὁ ἥλιος χύθηκε μέσα μου ἀπό χίλιες πληγές.
Καί τούτη τή λευκότητα πού σέ περιβάλλω
δέ θά τήν βρεῖς οὔτε στίς Ἄλπεις, γιατί αὐτός ὁ ἀγέρας
στριφογυρνᾶ ὥς ἐκεῖ ψηλά καί τό χιόνι λερώνεται.
Καί στό λευκό τριαντάφυλλο βρίσκεις μιά ἰδέα σκόνης.
Τό τέλειο θαῦμα θά τό βρεῖς μονάχα μές στόν ἄνθρωπο:
λευκές ἐκτάσεις πού ἀκτινοβολοῦν ἀληθινά
στό σύμπαν καί ὑπερέχουν. Τό πιό καθαρό
πρᾶγμα λοιπόν τῆς δημιουργίας δέν εἶναι τό λυκόφως,
οὔτε ὁ οὐρανός πού καθρεφτίζεται μές στό ποτάμι, οὔτε
ὁ ἥλιος πάνω στῆς μηλιᾶς τ᾽ ἄνθη. Εἶναι ἡ ἀγάπη.

Ἐπιτάφειο Ἐπίγραμμα

Σηκώνοντας στούς ὤμους του τό ἔπαθλο τοῦ Μαραθωνίου
ὁ ὡραῖος νεκρός κατεβαίνει στόν ἄδη,
᾽κεῖ πού οἱ αἰώνιοι Ἕλληνες τόν καρτεροῦν. Ἀλλ᾽ ὅμως
τούς πάει μισό τ᾽ ἄγγελμα:

ΝΕΝΙΚΗ—
ἄλλοι σᾶς φέρνουν πίσω μου τό ΝΕΝΙΚΗΚΑΜΕΝ.

Ἐγώ δέν ἤτανε νά ᾽ρθῶ τόσο ἐνωρίς, ἐμένα,
στῶν Πλαταιῶν τή χώρα καί τοῦ Μαραθώνα,
μέ σκοτώσανε οἱ Πέρσες.

There is no Solitude

There is no solitude where a man is
digging or whistling or washing his hands.
There is no solitude where a tree
stirs its leaves. Where an anonymous
insect finds a flower and sits,
where a brook is reflecting a star,
where holding his mother's breast
with his blissful little lips open
an infant sleeps, there is no solitude.

Ball State University *Forum,* XIX, No. 2 (Spring, 1978), 50.

Without You

Without you doves
wouldn't find water.

Without you God
wouldn't switch on the light in his fountains.

An apple tree sows its blossoms
in the wind; in your apron
you bring water from the sky
the glow of wheat, and above you

a moon of sparrows.

Seton Hall University
Spirit, XXXIV, No. 4 (Winter, 1972), 21.

Μοναξιά δέν ὑπάρχει

Μοναξιά δέν ὑπάρχει ἐκεῖ πού ἕνας ἄνθρωπος
σκάφτει ἤ σφυρίζει ἤ πλένει τά χέρια του.
Μοναξιά δέν ὑπάρχει ἐκεῖ πού ἕνα δέντρο
σαλεύει τά φύλλα του. 'Εκεῖ πού ἕνα ἀνώνυμο
ἔντομο βρίσκει λουλούδι καί κάθεται,
πού ἕνα ρυάκι καθρεφτίζει ἕνα ἄστρο,
ἐκεῖ πού βαστώντας τό μαστό τῆς μητέρας του
μ' ἀνοιγμένα τά δυό μακάρια χειλάκια του
κοιμᾶται ἕνα βρέφος, μοναξιά δέν ὑπάρχει.

Δίχως ἐσέ δέ θά 'βρισκαν

Δίχως ἐσέ δέ θά 'βρισκαν
νερό τά περιστέρια

Δίχως ἐσέ δέ θ' ἄναβε
τό φῶς ὁ Θεός στίς βρύσες του

Μηλιά σπέρνει στόν ἄνεμο
τ' ἄνθη της· στήν ποδιά σου
φέρνεις νερό ἀπ' τόν οὐρανό
φῶτα σταχυῶν κι' ἀπάνω σου

φεγγάρι ἀπό σπουργίτες.

Fever

When I go to town
I'll buy a horse
and a white sword
that'll reach the sun!
I'll gallop on the sea,
I'll climb up to the woods,
when I come back my
grace will fill the sky!

And one dawn, lowering
my body onto the saddle,
I'll go down to the plains
to save the world.

My little careless sisters,
my little careless sisters,
what a mindless dance
is that you've started?
under the white moon?
Get off the lilies,
the wind'll take you,
my little careless sisters!

Fairleigh Dickinson University *The Literary Review*, XVI,
No. 3 (Spring, 1973), 273.

Πυρετός

Σάν θά πάω στήν πόλη
θ' ἀγοράσω ἕνα ἄλογο
κι ἕν' ἄσπρο σπαθί
πού θά φτάνει ὡς τόν ἥλιο.
Θά καλπάζω στή θάλασσα,
θ' ἀνεβαίνω στό δάσος ...
Σάν γυρίζω, ἀπ' τή χάρη μου
θά γιομίζει ὁ οὐρανός.

Καί μι' αὐγή, χαμηλώνοντας
τό κορμί μου στή σέλλα,
θά κατέβω στούς κάμπους
νά σώσω τόν κόσμο!

'Αδελφοῦλες μου ἀπρόσεχτες,
ἀδελφοῦλες μου ἀπρόσεχτες!
Τί χορός ἀσυλλόγιστος
εἶν' αὐτός π' ἀρχινήσατε
κάτω ἀπ' τ' ἄσπρο φεγγάρι;
Κατεβῆτε ἀπ' τούς κρίνους,
θά σᾶς πάρει ὁ ἀγέρας,
ἀδελφοῦλες μου ἀπρόσεχτες!

If I Were

If I were to offer
you a lily
I would be adding
a stem
to the Evening Star.

from *Murky Rivers*

Love is the mountain
and the night with its stars.
Love is the sea
and the day with its sun.
And the little sparks
that fly from the chimney
of the house and the eyes
of the little bird even those
are love.

῎Αν ἦταν

῎Αν ἦταν νά σοῦ
προσφέρω ἕνα κρίνο
θά 'βαζα ἕναν
μίσχο
στόν ἕσπερο.

'Απ' τά Θολά Ποτάμια

'Αγάπη εἶναι τό βουνό
κι' ἡ νύχτα μέ τ' ἀστέρια της,
'Αγάπη εἶν' ἡ θάλασσα
κι' ἡ μέρα μέ τόν ἥλιο της.
Κι' οἱ μικρές σπίθες
πού βγαίνουν ἀπό τήν καπνοδόχο
τοῦ σπιτιοῦ καί τά μάτια
τοῦ μικροῦ πουλιοῦ ἀκόμα
εἶναι ἀγάπη.

The Strange Presence

As if God had molded you out of unused earth,
light and water, you are beautiful,
strangely so.

                                   Your hands resemble

an assembled people meditating
upon your breast. Your neck is a column
supporting a frieze. Your laugh
a peace camp. The sun alights
on you upright forehead, stangely.

                                        Your hair is

a tamed storm. And your eyes are
the wisdom of silence, the harmony of the storm,
the "love one another."

Seton Hall University *Spirit.* XXXIV, No 4 (Winter, 1972), 21.

Ἡ παράξενη παρουσία

Σά νά σ᾽ ἔπλασε ὁ Θεός μέ ἀμεταχείριστο χῶμα,
φῶς καί νερό, εἶσαι ὡραία
παράξενα.

                    Τά χέρια σου μοιάζουν
σάν ἔνας λαός συναγμένος πού σκέφτεται
πάνω στό στῆθος σου. Μιά κολώνα ὁ λαιμός σου
πού στηρίζει ἔνα ἀέτωμα. Μιά κατασκήνωση
εἰρήνης τό γέλιο σου. Στ᾽ ὀρθό μέτωπο σου,
προσγειώνεται ὁ ἥλιος παράξενα.
Τά μαλλιά σου εἶναι μιά
καταιγίδα πού ἡμέρωσε.

                    Καί τά μάτια σου εἶναι
ἡ σοφία τῆς σιωπῆς, ἡ ἁρμονία τῆς θύελλας, τό «ἀγαπᾶτε
                                        ἀλλήλους».

ARES DIKTAIOS

Beauty

Star that, when risen within us, never sets:
hovering in our innermost firmament like a sword
of justice against impositions coming from outside.
But if it loses its way upon our flesh,
it passes like a caress exposing us to strangers' eyes,
causes us pain, kills our sleep and, finally throws us
out, useless bones, to its faithful dog, death, who is awaiting.

University of Oklahoma, *Books Abroad,* 49, No. 2 (Spring, 1975), 368-369.

ZOË KARELLI

from *Diary* (122)

To begin life anew?

It isn't a matter of most beauteous
and ecstatic youth, not even one
of man's significant wisdom.

. . . .

Spirit and essence,
the complete presence,
reality and fantasy side by side.

University of Oklahoma, *Books Abroad,* 48, No. 4 (Fall, 1974), 827.

ΑΡΗΣ ΔΙΚΤΑΙΟΣ

Ὀμορφιά

Ἄστρο πού ἄν ἀνατείλη μέσα μας, δέ βασιλεύει:
στό ἐσώτερό μας στερέωμα αἰωρεῖται ὡς σπάθη
δικαιοσύνης ἐνάντια στίς ἐπιβουλές πού ἔρχονται ἀπ᾿ ἔξω.
Μ᾿ ἄν τό δρόμο της χάση στή σάρκα μας πάνω,
περνᾶ σάν χάδι πού στά ξένα μάτια μᾶς ἐκθέτει
καί μᾶς πονεῖ καί σκοτώνει τόν ὕπνο μας καί μᾶς πετᾶ, τέλος,
ἄχρηστο κόκκαλο, στό πιστό της σκυλί, τόν θάνατο, πού
περιμένει.

ΖΩΗ ΚΑΡΕΛΛΗ

ἀπό ῾Ημερολόγιο (122)

Νά ξαναρχίσεις τή ζωή;

Δέν πρόκειται γιά τήν περίκαλη
κι᾿ ἐκστατική νεότητα, οὔτε κάν
γιά τή γνώση τοῦ ἀνθρώπου τή σπουδαία.
. . . . . .
Πνεῦμα καί οὐσία,
ἡ πλήρης παρουσία,
πραγματικότητα καί φαντασία.

GEORGE KOTSIRAS

Biography
(Ezra Pound)

> "The poet Ezra Pound remains silent.
> He keeps his hands tightly clenched,
> occasionally snapping his fingers."
> (Newspaper interview)

Ezra Pound who had talked for so long
The words a river gushing from his heart
To glow like eyes of fish at the bottom
Now keeps silent, shut-up, and dim --

His red goatee now white like cotton
His old blue eyes watering

Shut-in behind the fence gate
He exchanges the ancient pentangle
For the cross with-the-broken-arms--

Alone he clenches his bony fingers
Joint by joint and snaps them like castanets

Silent, is he silent indeed?
"No!" shout the unconvinced:
"Alive he descended into Hell's porch
And has been arguing with Homer
In Dante's clearing --with an after-rain sun."

University of Oklahoma, *Books Abroad,* 50, No. 1 (Winter, 1976), 215.

ΓΙΩΡΓΗΣ ΚΟΤΣΙΡΑΣ

Βιογραφία

«Ὁ ποιητής Ἔζρα Πάουντ σωπαίνει.
Ἔχει δεμένα σφιχτά τά χέρια του κά-
νοντας πότε πότε στράκες μέ τά δά-
χτυλά του.»

Συνέντευξη σέ ἐφημερίδα

Ὁ Ἔζρα Πάουντ πού μίλησε τόσο πολύ
Τά λόγια ποταμός νά βγαίνουν ἀπό τό στῆθος
Νά φωσφορίζουν σάν μάτια ψαριῶν στό βυθό
Τώρα σωπαίνει μανταλωμένος καί σκοτεινός—

Τό κόκκινο γένι του ἄσπρο σάν τό βαμπάκι
Ψιχαλίζουν τά παλιά γαλάζια μάτια του

Κλεισμένος στήν καγκελόπορτα
Ξαλλάζει τήν ἀρχαία πεντάλφα
Μέ τό σταυρό σπασμένο σέ ἀγκύλες—

Μονάχος ἔχει δέσει τά ξερακιανά του δάχτυλα
Ἁρμό μέ ἁρμό καί τά χτυπᾶ σάν καστανιέτες

Σωπαίνει ἄραγε σωπαίνει ἀληθινά;
- Ὄχι φωνάζουν οἱ ἀμετάπειστοι:
Κατέβη ζωντανός στήν Ἀντικόλαση
Κι ἀντιλογιέται μέ τόν Ὅμηρο
Στό ξέφωτο τοῦ Δάντη—μέ ἥλιο ἀποβροχάρη.

DIMITRIS DOUKARIS

The Body of Ideas

If ideas have no real
body, if theories
have no
real life
then they are only phantoms
under false skin,
they are visions of the deceived,
delusions of those
who ran into adversity
and irrevocably missed
the live voices
of life-giving night;
where Rousing
awakes
unexpectedly,
and never rests
in delusion;
Rousing
of the real body
of ideas.

ΔΗΜΗΤΡΗΣ ΔΟΥΚΑΡΗΣ

Τό σῶμα τῶν ἰδεῶν

Ἄν δέν ἔχουν ἀληθινό σῶμα
οἱ ἰδέες, οἱ θεωρίες
ἄν δέν ἔχουν
πραγματική ζωή,
τότε εἶναι φαντάσματα
μέ ψεύτικο δέρμα,
εἶναι ὁράματα ἀπατημένων,
αὐταπάτες ἐκείνων
πού ἀτύχησαν
κι ἔχασαν ἀνεπίστρεπτα
τίς ζωντανές φωνές
τῆς ζωοδότρας νύχτας·
ἐκεῖ πού ἀφυπνίζεται
αἰφνιδιαστικά
ἡ Ἐξέγερση,
καί δέν ἐπαναπαύεται ποτέ
στήν αὐταπάτη·
ἡ Ἐξέγερση
τοῦ ἀληθινοῦ σώματος
τῶν ἰδεῶν.

TRIANDAFILLOS PITTAS

Deep Glance

Behind your hand coarse ambushes
Before your dream a colorless silence.

Acrid fruition of desire
you shoot the arrows of your hope
at the roses shedding their petals
at the dreams turned to ash.

Your hands fall off the wrists
your oars melt into the river
and when you reach the island in the middle of night
there is no calm by the fire
no coolness on the dead lips.

You spread your deep glance on the abyss
—a rising whirlwind in proud colors—
bending you pick a hidden pebble
the humblest, meekest, purest pebble.

You measure it in your expert palm
you feel its taste against your teeth
and throw it into the bottom of the well
awaiting the savage oracle
tearless, speechless, blind
into the echo of the night
into the wind of horror.

University of British Columbia, *PRISM International,* XIII, No. 2 (Winter, 1973), 97.

ΤΡΙΑΝΤΑΦΥΛΛΟΣ ΠΙΤΤΑΣ

Βλέμμα Βαθύ

Πίσω ἀπό τό χέρι σου ἐνέδρες βάναυσες
Ἐμπρός ἀπό τό ὄνειρό σου ἄχρωμη σιγή

Κάρπισμα στυφό τοῦ πόθου
ρίχνεις τά βέλη τῆς ἐλπίδας σου
ἀπάνω σέ ρόδα πού μαδοῦν
ἀπάνω στά ὄνειρα τῆς στάχτης

Τά χέρια σου πέφτουν πέρ᾽ ἀπό τόν καρπό
τά κουπιά σου λιώνουν στό ποτάμι
κι ὅταν φθάνεις στό νησί μεσονυχτίς
καμιά γαλήνη πλάι στήν πυροστιά
καμιά δροσιά στά μαραμένα χείλια.

Ἁπλώνεις τό βλέμμα σου βαθύ στήν ἄβυσσο
—στρόβιλος ἀνυψούμενος μέ περήφανα χρώματα—
διαλέγεις σκυφτός ἕνα βότσαλο κρυφό
τό πιό ταπεινό τό πιό πράο τό πιό ἀθῶο βότσαλο

Τό ἀναμετρᾶς στήν ἔμπειρη παλάμη σου
ὀσμίζεσαι τόν ἀχό του μέσα στά δόντια σου
καί τό ρίχνεις στό βάθος πηγαδιοῦ
καί περιμένεις τόν ἄγριο χρησμό
ἀδάκρυτος ἀμίλητος τυφλός
μέσα στῆς νύχτας τόν ἀντίλαλο
μέσα στόν ἄνεμο τῆς φρίκης.

Closed Room

The evening drowsed on the naked surfaces
dark folds on discolored garments
whispers from the winding paths
puffs of wind with the silence of cypress trees.

A naked leaf before the mirror
a silent word before itself

The closed room kneels in a friendly way
the temperature of the shadows goes up
the lamp light diminishes.

Marginal People

Subcutaneous insects guide us
into these cities whose backs are bent
by the will of the unclean.

Our lips are prisoners of vertigo
bloodstained daggers against our breath
subterranean pulses in profane blood.

Alone in the dressingrooms of remorse
Alone in the gloomy hopeless margin

No space no landscape around us
swaddled into a cocoon of scorn
we gather our body's dried sand
with no complaint, no tear, and no hope.

Ohio University *Mundus Artium,* VIII, No. 1 (1975), 142-3.

Κλειστό Δωμάτιο

Τό βράδι νύσταξε στίς γυμνές ἐπιφάνειες
σκοτεινές πτυχές στά ξεθωριασμένα ἐνδύματα
ψίθυροι ἀπό τά λοξά μονοπάτια
φυσήματα μέ τή σιωπή τῶν κυπαρισσιῶν

Ἕνα γυμνό φύλλο ἐμπρός στόν καθρέφτη
μιά σιωπηλή λέξη ἐμπρός στόν ἑαυτό της

Τό κλειστό δωμάτιο γονατίζει φιλικά
ἡ θερμοκρασία τῶν ἴσκιων ἀνεβαίνει
ἡ λάμπα χαμηλώνει

Οἱ Περιθώριοι

Ὑποδόρεια ἔντομα μᾶς ὁδηγοῦν
στίς πολιτεῖες τοῦτες πού καμπουριάζουν
ἀπό τή βούληση τῶν ρυπαρῶν

Τά χείλη μας αἰχμάλωτα στόν ἴλιγγο
ματωμένα ἐγχειρίδια στήν πνοή μας
ὑποχθόνιος σφυγμός στό βέβηλο αἷμα

Μόνοι στά ἀποδυτήρια τοῦ ὀνείρου
Μόνοι στό ζοφερό ἀνέλπιδο περιθώριο

Καμιά ἔκταση κανένα τοπίο γύρω μας
φασκιωμένοι σ' ἕνα βομβίκιο ἀπό χλεύη
μαζεύουμε τήν ἄργιλλο τοῦ κορμιοῦ μας
χωρίς παράπονο χωρίς δάκρυα χωρίς ἐλπίδα

The Epigraph

He went hiding into the garden of night flowers
behind the dark statues
into the cistern with the bats
he became a coalminer of the night.

(. . . he was looking for a new wine
for the delirium they had never heard)

Nothing
Nothing still
Nothing any longer

A rock only looming upright
an epigraph only, in chalk:
"Naked feet, crush him
dusty sandals, trample him
trample him . . ."

Nowhere

I heard your pulse travelling in the storm
I kissed your petal-plucking dream
I wrapped your cheek into the velvet of quiet

I asked the wind I invoked the sun
I awaited the echo of your shadows
I felt anguish facing the door of your escape

No finger sprinkled his down
no rain revealed its oracle
I found you nowhere, naked ones, in your immaterial
    garments.

Η Επιγραφή

Κρύφθηκε στόν κῆπο μέ τά νυχτολούλουδα
πίσω ἀπό τά μελανά ἀγάλματα
στή στέρνα μέ τίς νυχτερίδες
ἔγινε ἀνθρακωρύχος τῆς νύχτας

(. . . ἔψαχνε γιά ἕνα καινούριο κρασί
γιά τό παραλήρημα πού δέν ἄκουσαν ποτέ)

Τίποτε
Τίποτε ἀκόμη
Τίποτε πιά

Ἔνας βράχος μονάχα κατάκορφα
μιά ἐπιγραφή μονάχα μέ κιμωλία:
«Συνθλίψτε τον γυμνά πέλματα
πατῆστε τον σκονισμένα σανδάλια
πατῆστε τον. . .».

Πουθενά

Ἄκουσα τό σφυγμό σας νά ταξιδεύει σέ θύελλες
φίλησα τ' ὄνειρό σας πού μαδοῦσε πέταλα
τύλιξα τό μάγουλο σας μέ τό βελοῦδο τῆς σιγῆς.

Ρώτησα τόν ἄνεμο κάλεσα τόν ἥλιο
περίμενα τόν ἀντίλαλο τῶν ἴσκιων σας
ἀδημονοῦσα ἐμπρός στήν πόρτα τῆς φυγῆς σας

Κανένα δάχτυλο δέ ράντισε τά χνούδια του
καμιά βροχή δέ φανέρωσε τό χρησμό της
πουθενά δέ σᾶς βρῆκα, ὦ γυμνά, μέ τ' ἄϋλα ἐνδύματα.

KOSTES KOKOROVITS

Horses

1.
There are horses
Coming down the mountain
As the clouds touch them.
Black horses
And white
And grey ones.
They do not hurry
Nor gallop
Nor whinny.
They only pace slowly
Pensively
Majestically
And mournfully,
As if following
Royal funerals,
As if coming back
From lost battles.
As if lamenting
Invisible warriors
And knights
Of different times
Who were killed for Love,
As if walking the round
Of tread-mills,
As if forgotten
And left alone
In the waste land . . .

ΚΟΣΤΗΣ ΚΟΚΟΡΟΒΙΤΣ

Άλογα

1.
Εἶναι κάτι ἄλογα,
πού ἀπ' τό βουνό κατηφορίζουν,
καθώς τ' ἀγγίζουνε τά σύννεφα.
Άλογα μαῦρα
καί ἄσπρα
καί σταχτιά.
Δέν τρέχουνε
κι' οὐδέ καλπάζουνε
καί μήτε χλιμιντρᾶνε·
Μονάχα ἀργοπηγαίνουνε
στοχαστικά,
μεγαλόπρεπα
καί πένθιμα.
Σά ν' ἀκλουθᾶνε
κηδεῖες βασιληάδων,
σά νά ἐπιστρέφουν
ἀπό μάχες χαμένες
καί νά θρηνοῦν
πολέμαρχους ἀόρατους
καί ἱππότες
καιρῶν ἀλλοτινῶν
πού σκοτώθηκαν γιά τήν Ἀγάπη.
Σά νά στριφογυρίζουν
σέ μαγγανοπήγαδα,
σά ν' ἀποξεχάστηκαν
καί ξεμεῖναν
στήν ἐρμιά. . .

2.
There are horses
Coming and going
From the mountain,
Through the clouds,
Without horsemen.
But, as the night falls,
They get lost in it
Never appearing again;
And nobody knows
Nor asks why . . .

Vanderbilt University *Vanderbilt Poetry Review,* II, No. 1 (Fall/Winter, '75), 14-15.

2.

Εἶναι κάτι ἄλογα,
πού ἀπ' τό βουνό,
μέσ' ἀπ' τά σύννεφα,
πηγαίνουν
καί πᾶνε κι' ἔρχονται
δίχως καβαλλάρηδες.
Καί, καθώς νυχτώνει
χάνονται
καί ποτέ πιά δέν ξαναφαίνονται
καί δέν ξέρει κανείς
κ' οὔτε ρωτᾶ. . .

KOULA YIOKARINI

from *Tension of Time*

We leave in a light that can't be put out
Deserted
Among the crowds of those betrayed
Implacable we look at the graves
The ashes and the ruins.
Naked
We tremble under the cold eye
Of meditation.
The time to come
Won't be one of strife
It will only be a time of submission.

As if the heinous present weren't enough
We dig our children's graves
Into the brilliant future.

Vanderbilt University *Vandernilt Poetry Review,* II, No. 1
(Fall/Winter, 1975), 13.

ΚΟΥΛΑ ΓΙΟΚΑΡΙΝΗ

άπό τό ΅Ενταση Χρόνου

Μέ ἕνα ἄσβεστο φῶς φεύγουμε.
΅Ερημοι
μ' αὐτό τό πλῆθος τῶν προδομένων
κοιτάζουμε ἀδιάλλαχτοι τούς τάφους
τίς στάχτες καί τά ἐρείπια.
Γυμνοί
τρέμουμε κάτω ἀπ' τό κρύο μάτι
τῆς συλλογῆς.
῾Ο χρόνος πού θά ἔρθει
δέ θά εἶναι τῆς πάλης
παρά μόνο τῆς ὑποταγῆς.

Σά νά μήν ἔφτανε τό στυγερό παρόν
στά λαμπερά μέλλοντα
σκάβουμε τούς τάφους τῶν παιδιῶν μας.

PHILIP DRAKODAIDES

Pylades

My purpose was, following Orestes,
To lean my knife against the adulterers' hearts;
I even sought a certain special way,
Shouldering all responsibility vis-à-vis the Erinnyes.
I armed myself, in other words, with powerful sweetness,
Dissuading my friend from the sublime deed;
I followed him always having that one hope.
He surprised me, though, and while I was still
Thinking how to act, searching for something perfect,
He, in one stride, got inside the palace,
And did his work quickly, without considerations,
Nor delays of any kind; he'd had the knife at his side,
Leaving me completely unaware of his intentions.
I was much displeased by this behavior of his.
I hadn't seen him training before, in the past
But perhaps only once, inside that room of lawlessness
Where we lived together, merciless thinkers:
His voice had a hopeless shrillness
And underneath the carpet of inactivity that enveloped us.
He was talking, as a seer, of strange signs!
Ascending sentences: "I like to throw in the fire
Paper pipes and watch the flame go up,
Hissing, and sucking with its hook the live victim,
That soon turns black, bends, falls in a coma
And leaves the glow of dead sparkles
On its already wasted body. I'm training!"
Perhaps I should've set out on my own.

Finally I succeeded only in becoming
A certain dissonant echo of Orestes.

Fairleigh Dickinson University *The Literary Review,* XVI,
No. (Spring 1973), 321.

Φ. Δ. ΔΡΑΚΟΝΤΑΕΙΔΗΣ

Πυλάδης

Σκοπός μου ἦταν, ἀκολουθώντας τόν Ὀρέστη,
ν' ἀκουμπήσω τό μαχαίρι μου στίς καρδιές τῶν μοιχῶν·
καί μάλιστα ἀποζήτησα κάποιον ἰδιαίτερο τρόπο,
ἀναλαμβάνοντας ὅλες τίς εὐθύνες ἀπέναντι στίς Ἐρινύες.
Ὁπλίστηκα, θέλω νά πῶ, μέ ρωμαλέα ἡδύτητα,
ἀποτρέποντας τόν φίλο μου ἀπό τό θεσπέσιο τόλμημα·
τόν ἀκολούθησα μ' αὐτή πάντα τήν ἐλπίδα.
Ὅμως, μέ πρόλαβε κι ἐνῶ ἐγώ ἀκόμη σκεφτόμουν
νά κάμω ἔτσι ἤ ἀλλιῶς, ψάχνοντας γιά κάτι τέλειο,
αὐτός, μέ μιά δρασκελιά, μπῆκε στό μέλαθρο,
ἔκαμε τή δουλειά του γρήγορα, χωρίς ἀνασκοπές,
κανενός εἴδους χρονοτριβές, εἶχε τό μαχαίρι στό πλευρό
    του,
ἀφήνοντας ἐμένα, χωρίς κάν ὑποψία τῶν πράξεών του.
Πολύ μοῦ κακοφαίνεται τό φέρσιμό του αὐτό.
Δέν τόν εἶχα δεῖ παλαιότερα νά γυμνάζεται,
καμμιά φορά μονάχα, σ' ἐκεῖνο τό δωμάτιο τῆς παρανομίας,
ὅπου συγκατοικούσαμε, ἀνήλεοι στοχαστές,
ἡ φωνή του εἶχε μιά ἀπελπιστική ὀξύτητα
καί κάτω ἀπό τόν ἔρπητα τῆς ἀπραξίας πού μᾶς ἔζωνε,
μιλοῦσε, οἰωνοσκόπος στοιχείων παράξενων!
Φράσεις ἀνιοῦσες: «Μ' ἀρέσει νά ρίχνω στή φωτιά
ἕνα σωληνωτό χαρτί καί νά βλέπω τή φλόγα ν' ἀνεβαίνει,
νά σφυρίζει, νά ρουφάει μέ τό ἀγκιστρό της τό ζωντανό
    θύμα,
πού μαυρίζει γρήγορα, λυγίζει, πέφτει σέ κῶμμα
κι ἀφήνει ἀνταύγειες νεκρῶν σπινθήρων
στό σῶμα του, τριμμένο πιά. Ἐκπαιδεύομαι!»
Ἴσως ἐγώ νά χρειαζόταν νά εἶχα ξεκινήσει μόνος.

Τελικά δέν πέτυχα παρά νά γίνω
κάποια κακόηχη ἠχώ τοῦ Ὀρέστη.

Herakles

Three nights have passed
And midnight has yet to come.
Time was shot on contact
"Deceased while in service."

At home dishes, books, soiled clothes
Will be waiting for me
As well as quite a few neatness-machines;
And finally the smell of my activities
In the bed—satiation.

When of course midnight comes
I guess I'll bid the house farewell.

Sounds of bells, matins,
Dreams condensed into dreams: somewhere
Day must be breaking now, twilight.

With a strong push
I'll rid myself of the tables
And will strangle—an infant though I am—
The snakes that coil around my arms.

Ἡρακλῆς

Τρεῖς νύχτες περασμένες
καί τά μεσάνυχτα δέν φάνηκαν.
Ὁ χρόνος πυροβολήθηκε ἐξ ἐπαφῆς
«ἀπεβίωσε διατελῶν ἐν ὑπηρεσία».

Στό σπίτι θά μέ προσμένουν
πιάτα, βιβλία, ροῦχα ἄπλυτα
κι ἀρκετές μηχανές εὐπρεπισμοῦ·
καί τέλος ἡ μυρουδιά τῶν ἐνεργειῶν μου
στό κρεββάτι—κορεσμός.

Ὅταν βέβαια φανοῦν τά μεσάνυχτα
νομίζω ὅτι θ' ἀποχαιρετήσω τό σπίτι.

Φωνές καμπάνας, ὄρθροι,
ὄνειρα συμπυκνωμένα σ' ὄνειρα: κάπου
θά ξημερώνει τώρα, λυκαυγές.

Μ' ἕνα γερό σπρώξιμο
θ' ἀπαλλαγῶ ἀπό τά τραπέζια
καί θά πνίξω— σ' αὐτή τή νηπιακή ἡλικία—
τά φίδια πού μοῦ τυλίγουνε τά χέρια.

TAKIS ANTONIOU

from *The Revolution of the Dead*

I believe in one absurd living
almighty father of terror.
maker of God
and of all invisible shadows.
. . . .
Light from the sun's light
and darkness from the night's gloom
a true God,
plaything of coincidence
consubstantial to the earth
from which all was made.
. . . .
I long for my broken
fingers to hold
a minimum branch of an olive tree
in the present of endless time.

ΤΑΚΗΣ ΑΝΤΩΝΙΟΥ

ἀπό τήν 'Επανάσταση τῶν Νεκρῶν

'Εγώ πιστεύω σ' ἕνα παράλογο ζωντανό
παντοκράτορα πατέρα τοῦ τρόμου,
ποιητή τοῦ Θεοῦ
καί πάντων τῶν ἀοράτων σκιῶν.

. . . .

Φῶς ἀπ' τοῦ ἥλιου τό φῶς
καί σκότος ἀπ' τό ζόφο τῆς νύχτας
Θεό ἀληθινό,
παιχνίδι τῆς σύμπτωσης
ὁμοούσιο τῆς γῆς
δι' ἧς τά πάντα ἐγένετο.

. . . .

"Ενα κλαρί ἐλάχιστο ἐλιᾶς
λαχταρῶ νά κρατοῦν
τά σπασμένα μου δάκτυλα
στό παρόν τοῦ αἰῶνος χρόνου.

GEORGE THEMELIS

Naked Window

I thought of leaving this dead house
And going to live upon the sea
Shadows dwell in it forgotten voices
Disjointed dolls climb up and down the stairs

The window leans naked in the night
All the windowpanes have fallen
Pieces of glass upon the dust

And I stay and strive to find my shadow
Vestige of an old forgotten sun.

University of Iowa *Micromegas,* Greek Issue, V, No. 1 (1971), 27-8.

ΓΙΩΡΓΟΣ ΘΕΜΕΛΗΣ

Γυμνό παράθυρο

Εἶπα ν' ἀφήσω αὐτό τό πεθαμένο σπίτι
Νά πάω νά κατοικήσω ἐπάνω στή θάλασσα
Σκιές τό κατοικοῦν ξεχασμένες φωνές
'Εξαρθρωμένες κοῦκλες ἀνεβοκατεβαίνουν τίς σκάλες.

Τό παράθυρο γέρνει γυμνό μέσα στή νύχτα
"Ολα τά τζάμια ἔχουν πέσει
Κομμάτια ἀπό γυαλί πάνω στή σκόνη

Καί μένω κι ἀγωνίζομαι νά βρῶ τή σκιά μου
"Ιχνος ἀπό παλιό λησμονημένο ἥλιο.

TAKIS VARVITSIOTES

Idyll

Who has put the snow
To sleep
And it has remained forever pure
Like a grave

Who inhales
The eyelids of vapors

The white carnations
With their innocent lips

Down on earth the whirlwind
Swings
The shadows

The wedding gowns

The radiant face

A smile
Turned to grass

ΤΑΚΗΣ ΒΑΡΒΙΤΣΙΩΤΗΣ

Εἰδύλλιο

Ποιός ἀποκοίμησε
Τό χιόνι
Κι ἔμεινε ἀγνό γιά πάντα
Σάν ἕνας τάφος

Ποιός ἀνασαίνει
Τά βλέφαρα τῶν ἀτμῶν

Τ' ἄσπρα γαρύφαλλα
Μέ τ' ἀθῶα τους χείλη

Ὁ ἀνεμοστρόβιλος κάτω στή γῆ
Λικνίζει
Τούς ἴσκιους

Τά νυφικά φορέματα

Τό πρόσωπο μέ τίς ἀναλαμπές

Ἕνα χαμόγελο
Πού ἔγινε χλόη

A Mask of Wax

A mask of wax
against the black velvet
of celebration

A bird's voice drowning
in the bog of silence

A rosebay that makes
all faces disappear

And farther away beyond the roofs
the abyss of night
out of which her violet
absence emerges.

University of Oklahoma *World Literature Today,* vol. 55, No. 1
(Winter 1981).

Joined Hands

I touched your hand at the edge of night
And the river spoke to me
"Hurry, then, don't wait
For our words die
Faster than even a day"

You then looked at me
How blue your eyes were!

You are a shadow in bloom next to me
The silence I love

University of Oklahoma *World Literature Today,* vol. 55, No. 1
(Winter 1981).

Κέρινο προσωπείο

Ένα κέρινο προσωπείο
Πάνω στό μαῦρο βελοῦδο
Τῆς γιορτῆς

Μιά φωνή πουλιοῦ πού πνίγεται
Μέσα στό τέλμα τῆς σιωπῆς

Μιά ροδοδάφνη πού ἐξαφανίζει
Ὅλα τά πρόσωπα

Καί πιό πέρα ἀπ' τίς στέγες
Τό βάραθρο τῆς νύχτας
Ἀπ' ὅπου προβάλλει
Μενεξεδένια ἡ ἀπουσία της.

Ἑνωμένα χέρια

Ἔπιασα τό χέρι σου στήν ἄκρη τῆς νύχτας
Καί τό ποτάμι μοῦ μίλησε
«Βιάσου λοιπόν μήν περιμένεις
Γιατί τά λόγια μας πεθαίνουν
Πιό γρήγορα κι ἀπό τή μέρα»

Τότε μέ κοίταξες
Πόσο γαλάζια ἦταν τά μάτια σου!

Εἶσ' ἕνας ἴσκιος ἀνθισμένος πλάι μου
Ἡ σιωπή πού ἀγαπῶ

NIKOS ALEXIS ASLANOGLOU

Crude Oil

The buzzing of spring no longer overflows along
with my spirit. Scant and feeble it slides
among the tentacles of the lost correspondent.
The wind dries it up, the sea remains uncured.
It will never mingle with the sick bees
it no longer soaks my handkerchief, it doesn't
tolerate the ineffable force for a new life.

University of Oklahoma, *Books Abroad,* 50, No. 1 (Winter,
1976), 220.

ΝΙΚΟΣ ΑΛΕΞΗΣ ΑΣΛΑΝΟΓΛΟΥ

Ἀργό Πετρέλαιο

Ὁ θρόμβος τῆς ἄνοιξης δέν ξεχύνεται πιά
μέ τό πνεῦμα μου. Γλυστρᾶ λιγοστό καί ἀνίσχυρο
μές στούς πλοκάμους τοῦ χαμένου ἀνταποκριτῆ.
Ὁ ἄνεμος τό στεγνώνει, ἡ θάλασσα μένει ἀθεράπευτη.
Δέ θά σμίξει ποτέ μέ τίς ἄρρωστες μέλισσες
δέ διαβρέχει πιά τό μαντήλι μου, δέν ἀνέχεται
τήν ἀνέκφραστη δύναμη γιά καινούργια ζωή

GEORGE X. STOYANNIDES

The Fragments

With a clumsy move,
as I was shaving, I shattered the mirror
spraying myself with tiny
splinters of glass.
I am no longer alone, reflected by a myriad particles.
How long, though, will I bear this?
At times, I think that I am followed
by my dismembered limbs
and that frightens me.
It reminds me of those men in dark glasses
who watch your every move.

No, I prefer myself intact.

University of Oklahoma, *Books Abroad,* 49, No. 3 (Summer, 1975), 588.

ΓΕΩΡΓΙΟΣ Ξ. ΣΤΟΓΙΑΝΝΙΔΗΣ

Τά Θρύψαλα

Μέ μιά ἀδέξια κίνηση
ἔσπασα τόν καθρέφτη πού ξυριζόμουν
γεμίζοντας τό κορμί μου μικρά μικρά
γυάλινα θρύψαλα.
Δέν εἶμαι πιά μόνος, καθρεφτισμένος σ' ἄπειρα μόρια
χαίρομαι τ' ὀδυνηρό μου κομμάτιασμα.
῎Ομως πόσο θ' ἀντέξω;
Κάποτε, θαρῶ πώς μέ παρακολουθοῦν
τά διαμελισμένα μου μέλη
κι αὐτό μέ τρομάζει.
Μοῦ θυμίζει ἐκείνους μέ τά μαῦρα γυαλιά
πού ἐλέγχουν τήν κάθε σου κίνηση.

῎Οχι, προτιμῶ τόν ἀκέραιο ἑαυτό μου.

DINOS CHRISTIANOPOULOS

Antigone's Defense of Oedipus

Men of Athens, why do you view us with curiosity?
This is my father Oedipus,
who was once a famous king and now
wanders in your marketplace stricken
by destiny, blind, and in rags,
grinding his decrepit little organ.

Men of Athens, each of your obols
adds to our hearts one more crack;
the secrets of our House grow heavier
with the additions of your own imaginations.
Leave us alone, how long will you keep
dragging us here and there, like a gypsy and his bear;
how long will you keep putting us on stage,
besieging us for more details
and asking how this ever happened,
how he didn't manage to avoid it?

Men of Athens, aren't you satisfied
that my father was once a poet,
the first one to introduce symbolism,
who, with the epigramme "Answer to the Sphinx",
saved many of your lives – apart
from the aesthetic pleasure offered?
why do you intrude into his private life
and search for oedipal complexes,
illicit loves,
and pleasures that current morality forbids?

The "Answer to the Sphinx" should have sufficed you.
The rest you could have left in half-darkness.
For, after all, he did it unawares;
whereas you do it in full conscience.

ΝΤΙΝΟΣ ΧΡΙΣΤΙΑΝΟΠΟΥΛΟΣ

Ἀντιγόνης ὑπέρ Οἰδίποδος

Ἄνδρες Ἀθηναῖοι, τί μᾶς κοιτᾶτε μέ περιέργεια;
Αὐτός εἶν' ὁ πατέρας μου, ὁ Οἰδίποδας,
πού κάποτε ἦταν βασιλιᾶς τρανός καί τώρα
γυρνάει στήν ἀγορά σας πληγωμένος
ἀπό τή μοῖρα, κουρελιάρης καί τυφλός,
παίζοντας μέ τό χαλασμένο του ὀργανάκι.

Ἄνδρες Ἀθηναῖοι, κάθε ὀβολός σας
προσθέτει στήν καρδιά μας μιά ραγισματιά.
Τοῦ οἴκου μας τά μυστικά βαραίνουν
ἀπ' τῆς δικῆς σας φαντασίας τίς προσθῆκες
Ἀφῆστε μας, ὡς πότε θά μᾶς σέρνετε
ἐδῶ καί κεῖ, σά γύφτο μέ ἀρκούδα—
κι οἱ τραγοδοί νά μᾶς ἀνεβάζουν στά θέατρα,
νά μᾶς πολιορκοῦν, γιά λεπτομέρειες
καί νά ρωτοῦν πῶς γίνηκε αὐτό,
πῶς δέν κατάφερε τό χτύπημα ν' ἀποφύγει.

Ἄνδρες Ἀθηναῖοι, δέ σᾶς φτάνει
πού ὁ πατέρας μου ὑπῆρξε ποιητής,
ὁ πρῶτος τοῦ συμβολισμοῦ εἰσηγητής,
πού μέ τό ἐπίγραμμα «Ἀπάντηση στή Σφίγγα»
ἔσωσε τή ζωή πολλῶν σας—χώρια
ἡ αἰσθητική ἀπόλαυση· γιατί
στόν ἰδιωτικό του βίο εἰσδύετε
καί ψάχνετε γιά οἰδιπόδεια συμπλέγματα,
ἄνομους ἔρωτες
καί ἡδονές πού ἀπαγορεύει ἡ τρεχάμενη ἠθική;

Σᾶς ἔφτανε ἡ «Ἀπάντηση στή Σφίγγα».
Τ' ἄλλα ἄς τ' ἀφήνατε στό μισοσκόταδο.
Στό κάτω κάτω, τό 'κανε ἐν ἀγνοίᾳ του
ἐνῶ ἐσεῖς τό κάνετε ἐν πλήρει γνώσει.

PANOS THASITES

Home on Earth

A cheerful house can be seen
white with a red roof, a well and vegetable garden.
The earth deposits in it the secret of its fragrance;
a forest colt licks its wooden threshold at night;
he also brings the secret of his simple life.
The stars come low, lured into the sleepless water.
We can live here.

The river flows near by
through reeds and bushes which have no name,
through rushes that offer with love whatever they have,
it flows by us and hardly notices us.
It washes the feet of birds, quenches the thirst of horses,
waters—as best it can—the fields.
It has no tales nor dreams at night;
it is water
it does its work well
it gets tired
it sleeps.

University of Iowa *Micromegas,* Greek issue, V, No. 1 (1971)
27-8.

ΠΑΝΟΣ ΘΑΣΙΤΗΣ

Κατοικία στή γῆ

Διαγράφεται σπίτι χαρωπό
ἄσπρο μέ κόκκινη στέγη, μέ πηγάδι καί λαχανόκηπο.
Ἡ γῆ ἀποθέτει μέσα του τῆς εὐωδιᾶς της τό μυστικό·
πουλάρι τοῦ δρυμοῦ γλύφει τό ξύλινο κατώφλι του τίς
νύχτες,
φέρνει κι αὐτό τό μυστικό τῆς ἁπλῆς του ζωῆς·
τ' ἄστρα χαμηλώνουν, ἕλκονται μές στό νερό πού ἀγρυπνεῖ.
Μποροῦμε νά κατοικήσουμε.

Τό ποτάμι περνάει ἀπ' ἐδῶ
μές ἀπό καλαμιές καί θάμνους πού ὄνομα δέν ἔχουν,
μές ἀπό χόρτα πού προσφέρουν μ' ἀγάπη ὅ,τι ἔχουν,
περνάει κι ἀπό μᾶς καί δέν μᾶς ξεχωρίζει.
Πλένει τά πόδια τῶν πουλιῶν, τ' ἄλογα ξεδιψάει,
ποτίζει—ὅσο μπορεῖ—τά χωράφια.
Δέν ἔχει θρύλους μήτε ὄνειρα τά βράδια·
εἶναι νερό
κάνει καλά τή δουλειά του
κουράζεται
κοιμᾶται.

They Should've Given In A Little

What do these people want now, and get us angry?
What's this nonsense they mouth again about, supposedly
    hazy deals
And unlawful gains?

They are rude and envious, third-generation paupers,
Starving —and rightly so, considering who they are—
They don't even know what life means
—They take it easy, begging for a living—
And now they pretend to be righteous,
They act like a bunch of Robespierres!

After all, they too should've been enterprizing,
Should've given in a little, should've been flexible a bit,
Should've seized opportunities, should've pushed and stepped
        on others when needed
After all, nobody has ever forbidden these things
—All of us manage to live with them and make do.

Are they posing to us as wise guys, now?

Ἂς Ὑποχωροῦσαν Λίγο

Τί θέλουν τώρα αὐτοί καί μᾶς θυμώνουν;
Τί κουταμάρες λένε πάλι γιά δῆθεν ὕποπτους συνδυασμούς
γι' ἀνόμως κερδισμένα;

Εἶναι ζηλιάρηδες, ἀνάγωγοι, ξυπόλητοι πάππου πρός
πάππον,
πεινασμένοι—καί δικαίως τέτοιοι πού' ναι—
δέν ξέρουν τί θά πεῖ ζωή
—τήν πήρανε στά εὔκολα ψωμοζητώντας—
καί τώρα κάνουν τούς ἐνάρετους,
παίζουν τούς Ροβεσπιέρους!

Στό κάτω - κάτω, ἄν ἦταν ἱκανοί κι αὐτοί,
ἄς ὑποχωροῦσαν λίγο, ἄς ἑλίσσονταν λιγάκι,
ἄς ἅρπαζαν τίς εὐκαιρίες, ἄς σπρῶχναν κι ἄς πατοῦσαν στήν
ἀνάγκη
ἀφοῦ κανείς δέν τ' ἀπαγόρεψε αὐτά
—ὅλοι μέ κάτι τέτοια ζοῦμε καί περνοῦμε

Τούς ἔξυπνους μᾶς κάνουν τώρα;

ANESTIS EVANGELOU

The Poet

He had climbed to the highest peak
his voice, a white bird in the sky.
A huge crowd swarmed in the foothills.
Hearing his voice that kept climbing,
the circle was getting narrower,
they were holding clubs,
knives and stones, they were getting closer.
Shouts were heard, *"kill him"*;
the first stones began to fly;
knives shone against the sun
he sensed that this was the end.

But his voice,
a white bird was flying above their heads
and shouts and knives couldn't reach him.

The Heavy Knife

When the heavy knife fell
and cut the deep wound in my chest
I couldn't, of course, understand its meaning:
time had to complete its flow.

Since then I've learned and suffered much
— mostly this: that I had to get accustomed
to loving the wound,
to loving the heavy knife.

Reprinted in Pitzer College
Grove: Contemporary Poetry and Translation, No. 5 (Winter.
1979), 44.

ΑΝΕΣΤΗΣ ΕΥΑΓΓΕΛΟΥ

Ὁ ποιητής

Εἶχε ἀνεβεῖ στήν πιό ψηλή κορφή
κι ἡ φωνή του, λευκό πουλί στόν οὐρανό.
Στούς πρόποδες μυρμήγκιαζε πλῆθος ἀμέτρητο
ἄκουγαν τή φωνή κι ὁλοένα ἀνέβαιναν
μίκραινε ὁ κύκλος καί κρατοῦσαν ξύλα
μαχαίρια κράταγαν καί πέτρες καί πλησίαζαν
ἀκούγονταν κραυγές σκοτῶστε τον
νά πέφτουν ἄρχισαν μετά οἱ πρῶτες πέτρες
λάμψαν στόν ἥλιο τά μαχαίρια
κατάλαβε τό τέλος του.

Ὅμως ἡ φωνή του,
λευκό πουλί πέταγε πάνω ἀπ' τά κεφάλια τους
καί δέν τή φτάναν οἱ κραυγές καί τά μαχαίρια.

Τό βαρύ μαχαίρι

Ὅταν ἔπεσε τό βαρύ μαχαίρι
καί μοῦ ἄνοιξε τή βαθιά πληγή πού ἔχω στό στῆθος
δέ μποροῦσα, βέβαια, νά καταλάβω τή σημασία του:
ἔπρεπε ὁ χρόνος νά διαγράψει τήν τροχιά του.

Ἔκτοτε ἔπαθα καί ἔμαθα πολλά—κυρίως
αὐτό: πῶς πρέπει πλέον νά συνηθίσω,
νά ἀγαπήσω τήν πληγή
νά ἀγαπήσω τό βαρύ μαχαίρι.

The First Steps

My friend, to get in here you've got to be distinguished
to have great imagination, to be an artist.
It's a delicate, scientific and difficult job,
take it from me with my whitened hair.

In the beginning, of course, it's a bit hard:
screams pierce the eardrums

                                  and blood,
warm and red, hurts your eyes.

                                  Well then:
this is the crucial, the important moment:
most people give up then and leave.

Few stay. You yourself
look good to me, you'll go places - -
your eyes are gleaming.
When, with the passing of time, you mature
and become an expert in devices,
when you refine your art and cleanse it
of the stain of your latest hesitation
and art remains for art's sake —
remember me: it hides great delights.

And now, come for me to show you one by one
the tools of our trade and their uses.

This pair of pincers is meant for fingernails.
You see, quite blunt at its jaws
so it won't clip them; made to order.
You get hold of the fingernail,
you press it hard and pull it.

                                  Wonderful
tool, most handy.

Τά πρῶτα βήματα

Φίλε μου, ἐδῶ γιά νά 'μπεις πρέπει νά 'σαι ἐκλεκτός.
νά 'χεις μεγάλη φαντασία, νά 'σαι καλλιτέχνης.
Εἶναι λεπτή, ἐπιστημονική καί δύσκολη δουλειά,
στό λέω ἐγώ πού ἀσπρίσαν τά μαλλιά μου.

Στήν ἀρχή, βέβαια, εἶναι λιγάκι δύσκολο:
τρυποῦν τά τύμπανα οἱ κραυγές
                                        καί τό αἷμα,
ζεστό καί κόκκινο, τά μάτια σου πληγώνει.
                                        Λοιπόν,
ἐδῶ εἶν' ἡ κρίσιμη στιγμή, ἡ μεγάλη:
οἱ πιό πολλοί τά παρατοῦν καί φεύγουν.

Μένουνε λίγοι. Ἐλόγου σου
μοῦ φαίνεσαι καλός, θά προοδέψεις—
λάμπουν τά μάτια σου.
Ὅταν, μέ τοῦ καιροῦ τό πέρασμα, ὡριμάσεις
καί γίνεις ἄσος στίς ἐπινοήσεις,
ὅταν τήν τέχνη σου ἐκλεπτύνεις καί τήν καθαρίσεις
ἀπ' τή βρωμιά τοῦ τελευταίου σου δισταγμοῦ
καί μείνει ἡ τέχνη γιά τήν τέχνη—
θυμήσου με: κρύβει μεγάλες ἡδονές.

Καί τώρα, ἔλα νά σοῦ δείξω ἕνα ἕνα
τά ἐργαλεῖα τῆς δουλειᾶς μας καί τή χρήση τους.

Αὐτή ἡ τανάλια εἶναι γιά τά νύχια.
Βλέπεις, διόλου κοφτερή στίς ἄκρες
ὥστε νά μήν τά κόβει· εἰδική
παραγγελία. Πιάνεις γερά τό νύχι,
τό σφίγγεις δυνατά καί τό τραβᾶς.
                                        Θαυμάσιο
ἐργαλεῖο, πρακτικό.

137

This one here is the "screwer."
Yes, yes, like the one they thrust screwing
into the cork of a wine bottle,
only a bit sharper. You thrust it sharply
into the flesh, without your hand
shaking on account of ridiculous deferments
—of course, you'll develop this skill with experience—
you screw it gently until you reach the bone.

Here's the "branding iron." One of the finest
tools of the trade. With a wooden, pretty
handle to hold it from,
and a steel blade, glistening.

                                          When it gets hot

and turns red by the fire,
you carve the body, and if
your hand is firm, you can make patterns:
so perfect it is.

Finally, there are other means, of course: electroshock,
hallucinogenics — the latest
word in our technology — we've got
contraptions of unbelievable subtlety and precision.

                                          With patience

and in time, you'll master all of them.

The Coffeehouse, No. 3 (Fall, 1976), 23-26.

Ἐτοῦτο ἐδῶ εἶν' οἱ "στρίφτης".
Ναί, ναί, καθώς ἐκεῖνο πού βυθίζουν στρίβοντάς το
στό πῶμα τῆς φιάλης τοῦ κρασιοῦ,
μόνο, πιό κοφτερό, κομμάτι. Τό μπήγεις
ἀπότομα στή σάρκα καί χωρίς
τό χέρι σου νά τρέμει ἀπό γελοῖες ἀναστολές
—αὐτό θά τό κερδίσεις, βέβαια, μέ τήν πείρα—
τό στρίβεις λίγο λίγο ὥσπου στό κόκαλο νά φτάσεις.

Νά κι ὁ "σημαδευτής". Ἀπ' τά πιό φίνα
σύνεργα τῆς δουλειᾶς. Μέ ξύλινη,
ὡραία λαβή, γιά νά τόν πιάνεις,
κι ἀτσάλινη λεπίδα, ἀστραφτερή.

                              Μόλις πυρώσει
καί γίνει κόκκινος ἀπ' τή φωτιά,
χαράζεις τό κορμί, κι ἄν πιάνει
καί τό χέρι σου, μπορεῖς καί σχέδια νά κάμεις:
τόσο τέλειος εἶναι.

Τέλος, εἶναι καί ἄλλα βέβαια: ἠλεκτροσόκ,
παραισθησιογόνα—ἡ τελευταία
λέξη τῆς τεχνικῆς μας—ἔχουμε συσκευές
ἀπίθανης λεπτότητος καί ἀκριβείας.

                              Ὅμως αὐτά,
μέ τήν ὑπομονή καί μέ τό χρόνο θά τά μάθεις.

The Light

Even into the darkest burrows
the deepest
the most forgotten ones,
sometimes
as if in an intermission
and when nobody expects anything any longer,
miraculous
comforting
comes the light.

University of Oklahoma *World Literature Today,* 51, No. 2
(Spring, 1977).

Τό φῶς

Καί στά πιό σκοτεινά λαγούμια
τά πιό βαθιά
τά πιό λησμονημένα
ἔρχεται κάποτε
ὡσάν σέ διάλειμμα
κι ὅταν κανείς πιά τίποτε δέν περιμένει
θαυματουργό
παρήγορο
τό φῶς.

CYPRIOT POEMS

KYPROS CHRYSANTHIS

Lefkosia (Nicosia) a Sonnet

For miracles and a flood is the time,
Of commemorative lamps the rosy flames;
And, Lefkosia, the twilight frames
Your sky like a fate sublime.

Your castles were filled by an ancient tale,
Much as for flowers the bees of spring
Blessings and perfumes bring
Such as the prayers of a maiden unveil.

Come, empty the jug, stranger-friend,
Filled with the rosy-grape wish.
Cyprus' pride is this stead.

As if for a beautiful archaic head,
O friend, the hymn for our isle finish,
That's blooming, no longer wilted by conquerors' tread.

The Charioteer, Nos. 7-8 (1965), 32-33, 38.

ΚΥΠΡΟΣ ΧΡΥΣΑΝΘΗΣ

Λευκωσία

Γύρα θαμμάτων ὥρα καί πλημμύρα,
λύχνων θυμητικῶν ροδάτη φλόγα,
κι ὦ Λευκωσία, τό δείλι ἐκορφολόγα
τόν οὐρανό σου σά θαυμάσια μοῖρα.

Θρύλος παλιός τά κάστρα σου ἐπλημμύρα
καθώς μελίσι σέ ἄνοιξη πού εὐλόγα
λεπτούς ἀνθούς, καί ξάμωναν τά μύρα
γύρα σά νέας παράκληση ἀνθολόγα.

᾿Ω ξένε, ἐδῶ τό κύπελλο ν᾽ ἀδειάσω
μέ τήν εὐχή τήν τριανταφυλλορόγα.
᾿Εδῶ τῆς Κύπρου βρίσκεται τ᾽ ἀφάλι.

Τόν ὕμνο, σά γιά ὡραῖο κι᾽ ἀρχαῖο κεφάλι
γιά τό νησί μας, ξένε, νά ξοδιάσεις,
π᾽ ἀνθεῖ, ἀπ᾽ τούς ξένους ἄν κι ἐφυλλορόγα.

MANOS KRALIS

Sea Monument

The dark mirror of the stars
Cracks at the touch of their finger-tips.

They are forgotten in the eyes of a mermaid
In the yellow, dead south seas.

Armfuls of lilies, the meek pigeons
Stir and tap their wings over the vernal tomb.

Egyptian dew of the Morning Star on their hair,
They drink the light of Berenice at the end of the world.

Nights we loved, Matis, Antony, and Vitsko,
On what remote shores are they breaking?

The sob from the plucked shrouds,
The shadow of a keel, sweeten your dream.

At midnight, in the golden gardens of death
I expect destiny from your buried lips:

A hand that freezes in a hand; and our wound
A withered rose.

The Charioteer, Nos. 7-8 (1965), 32-33, 38.

ΜΑΝΟΣ ΚΡΑΛΗΣ

Θαλασσινό Μνημεῖο

«Τό Γιουγκοσλαυϊκό φορτηγό «Shebreno»
ναυάγησε στίς θάλασσες τοῦ Νότου».

Στά γυμνά ἀκροδάχτυλα, κλαίει καί ραγίζει
ὁ σκοτεινός τῶν ἀστεριῶν καθρέφτης.

Στίς κίτρινες τίς πεθαμμένες θάλασσες τοῦ νότου
μές τά χρυσᾶ τά μάτια μιᾶς γοργόνας ξεχαστῆκαν.

Ἀγκαλιές τά κρῖνα, πράα περιστέρια
στή χλωρή ταφόπετρα κινοῦν καί φτερουγίζουν.

Μέ τή δροσό τῆς πούλιας, στούς λυτούς βοστρύχους
στήν ἄκρηα τοῦ κόσμου ἤπιανε τό φῶς τῆς Βερενίκης.

Μάτις, Ἀντονύ καί Βίτσκο, νύκτες π' ἀγαπήσαμε
σέ ποιές ἀλαργινότατες ἀκτές νά κυματίζουν;

Ἀπ' τά μαδημένα ξάρτια, ὁ λυγμός γλυκαίνει
ἀντάμα μέ τόν ἴσκιο μιᾶς καρίνας τ' ὄνειρό σας.

Τό μεσονύχτι στούς χρυσούς τούς κήπους τοῦ θανάτου
ἀπ' τό θαμμένο ἀχείλι σας, τή Μοῖρα περιμένω

—Τό χέρι νά ξυλιάζει μές τό χέρι, κι' ἡ πληγή μας
σάμπως λησμονημένο ρόδο νἆναι!...

PETROS SOPHAS

Resolution

You've gathered all the patience
From the beggars' trays
And have tied it a knot in your handkerchief.
You've sat so many times
At the threshold of Spring
Hearing but the same dirge.
You were looking at the sky
For hours on end so many nights
With no star filling your palm.
What are you still waiting for?
Take the beggars' empty trays
And make them a tambourine.
Take a sound from the dirge of Spring
And make the song of Tomorrow.
Tighten your empty hand
And strike to open your way.

The Charioteer, Nos. 7-8 (1965), 38-39.

ΠΕΤΡΟΣ ΣΟΦΑΣ

Ἀπόφαση

Μάζεψες ὅλη τήν ὑπομονή
ἀπό τούς δίσκους τῶν ζητιάνων
καί τήν ἔδεσες κόμπο στό μαντήλι σου.
Κάθησες τόσες φορές
στό κατώφλι τῆς Ἄνοιξης
μά δέν ἄκουσες παρά τόν ἴδιο θρῆνο.
Κοίταξες ὦρες ἀτέλειωτες
τόν οὐρανό τόσες νύκτες
χωρίς ἕν' ἀστέρι νά γεμίσει τή φούχτα σου.

Τί περιμένεις ἀκόμα;
Πάρε τούς ἄδειους δίσκους τῶν ζητιάνων
καί κάνε τους ντέφι.
Πάρε ἕναν ἦχο ἀπό τό θρῆνο τῆς Ἄνοιξης
καί φτιάξε τό τραγούδι τοῦ Αὔριο.
Σφίξε τήν ἄδεια σου φούχτα
καί κτύπα ν' ἀνοίξῃς τό δρόμο σου.

YIANNIS K. PAPADOPOULOS

Let's Say

Let's say that now we are first facing the light of the world,
    That our ships never set sail for Troy
    And the Mycenean kings didn't go hunting lions,
    For the artisans to engrave their golden memories on the
        metal of immortality.
Let's say that the Persians haven't yet come
    To ask for our land
    And the buzzards at Marathon haven't counted their
        bodies
    And the shells in the sea of Salamis
    Haven't clung to the sunken triremes;
    That Pheidias' hands
    Are the tiny hands of this newborn baby
    Awaited by the unwrought marbles of our country.

Let's say that the masterpieces of Aeschylus and Sophocles
    Are still these bright sparks
    In the eyes of the youth who passes by;
    That the golden age is that fair wheat
    We sow in sweat with the vision of Threshing;
    That the leaves of this wild olive tree we are now grafting
    Will some day shine like silver
    At the flowering of Platonic thought.
Let's say that now we are first facing the light of the world
And let's say only that the others call us Greeks.

The Charioteer, Nos. 7-8 (1965), 38-39.

ΓΙΑΝΝΗΣ Κ. ΠΑΠΑΔΟΠΟΥΛΟΣ

Ἄς Ποῦμε

Ἄς ποῦμε πώς τώρα πρωτοβγαίνουμε στό φῶς τοῦ κόσμου,
πώς τά καράβια μας ποτέ δέν ἄνοιξαν πανιά γιά τήν Τροία
κι' οἱ Μυκηναῖοι βασιλιάδες δέ βγῆκαν σέ κυνήγι
    λιονταριῶν,
σέ μέταλλο ἀθανασίας οἱ τεχνίτες νά χαράξουν τή χρυσή
    τους μνήμη.
Ἄς ποῦμε πώς δέν ἦρθαν ἀκόμα οἱ Πέρσες
νά ζητήσουν τή γῆ μας
καί τά ὄρνια τοῦ Μαραθῶνα δέν μετρήσανε τά κορμιά τους
καί τά κοχύλια στά νερά τῆς Σαλαμίνας
δέν κολλήσανε στίς βουλιαγμένες τους τριήρεις.
Πώς τά χέρια τοῦ Φειδία εἶναι
αὐτά τά χεράκια τοῦ νιογέννητου βρέφους
πού τά προσμένουν τ' ἄπλαστα μάρμαρα τοῦ τόπου μας.
Ἄς ποῦμε πώς τ' ἀριστουργήματα τοῦ Αἰσχύλου καί τοῦ
    Σοφοκλῆ
εἶναι ἀκόμα αὐτές οἱ λαμπερές σπίθες
στά μάτια τοῦ ἐφήβου πού περνᾶ,
πώς ὁ χρυσός αἰώνας εἶναι αὐτό τό ξανθό σιτάρι
πού σπέρνουμε ἱδροκοπῶντας μέ τ' ὄραμα τοῦ Θερισμοῦ.
Πώς αὐτῆς τῆς ἀγρελιᾶς πού μπολιάζουμε
θ' ἀσημοτρέμουν τά φύλλα μιά μέρα
στό ἄνθισμα ἑνός Πλατωνικοῦ στοχασμοῦ.
Ἄς ποῦμε πώς τώρα πρωτοβγαίνουμε στό φῶς τοῦ κόσμου
κι' ἄς ποῦμε μόνο πώς μᾶς λένε οἱ ἄλλοι: Ἕλληνες.

NADINA DIMITRIOU

from *Snap-Shots I*

The will isn't asleep, when faith is watchful
and waste lands are besieged
by swallow chirpings and cloud shadows.

A time comes when palid faces
born like winter dawns
turn into water,
and their thoughts raise fruitful
the curves of labor.

* * * * * *

The sounds of steps
Are they echoes of self-mastered thought?

* * * * * *

The insignificant causes the rift
and insincerity is its reason.

* * * * * *

Too bad the morning magic
goes to waste
amidst conventional smiles
and a voice doing acrobatics.

The morning magic
—in a child's awakening.

* * * * * *

Our friends! . . . Who are they?
A polyphony wedged
into a wall of the heart.

ΝΑΔΙΝΑ ΔΗΜΗΤΡΙΟΥ

ἀπό τά Στιγμιότυπα

Δέν κοιμᾶται ἡ βούληση, ὅταν ἡ πίστη ἀγρυπνᾶ
καί πολιορκοῦνται οἱ ἐρημιές
ἀπό χελιδονίσματα καί συννεφιῶν σκιές.

Χλωμές μορφές πού γεννιοῦνται σά χειμωνιάτικες αὐγές
ἔρχεται ἡ ὥρα πού γίνονται πηγές
κι οἱ λογισμοί τους, ἀναστήνουν
καρποφόρες τοῦ μόχθου καμπύλες.

* * * * * *

Οἱ βηματισμοί
ἀντίλαλοι αὐτεξούσιας σκέψης·

* * * * * *

Τ' ἀσήμαντο ἡ ἀφορμή γιά τή ρωγμή
κι ἀνειλικρίνεια ἡ αἰτία.

* * * * * *

Ἡ μαγεία τοῦ πρωινοῦ
Τί κρίμα νά ξοδεύεται
ἀνάμεσα σέ συμβατικά χαμόγελα
καί φωνή π' ἀκροβατεῖ.

Ἡ μαγεία τοῦ πρωινοῦ
στοῦ παιδιοῦ τό ξύπνημα.

* * * * * *

Οἱ φίλοι μας! . . . Ποιοί εἶναι;
Μιά πολυφωνία σφηνωμένη
σ' ἕνα τοῖχο τῆς καρδιᾶς.

Passions solidify,
as layers of rocks
tell the story of an evolution.

* * * * * *

The hours of silence have no price
Hours that teach you to love
whatever is worth, in the manner it is worth
wherever you are, whatever you have become.

Pitzer College, *Grove: Contemporary Poetry and Translation,*
No. 5 (Winter, 1979), 60.

Idyll

A light blue hue
and coolness run away
from a ravine
toward an idyll.

Mountain slopes, fields
are witnesses
shallow roots on the surface
are paths
and labyrinthine shadows
are nests.

And the sun talks softly
to memory, panting
when the lips turn upwards,
when the eyelids consent.

University of British Columbia, *PRISM International,* XIII,
No. 2 (Spring, 1973), 110-111; and, University of Oklahoma,
Books Abroad, 47, No. 4 (Fall, 1973), 809.

Τά πάθη πήζουν.
Τῶν πετρωμάτων στρώματα
ἐξιστοροῦνε μιά ἐξέλιξη.

* * * * * *

Οἱ ὧρες τῆς σιωπῆς εἶναι ἀνεκτίμητες.
Ὧρες πού σοῦ μαθαίνουν ν' ἀγαπᾶς
ὅ,τι ἀξίζει, ὅπως ἀξίζει
ὅπου κι ἄν εἶσαι, ὅ,τι κι ἄν ἔχης γίνει.

Εἰδύλλιο

Ἀπό ρεματιά
Γαλάζιο καί δροσιά
γιά ἕνα εἰδύλλιο
δραπετεύουν.

Βουνοπλαγιές, ἀγροί
οἱ μάρτυρες
ρηχά ριζοβολήματα
τά μονοπάτια
κι οἱ πολυδαίδαλες σκιές
φωλιές.

Κι ἕνας ἥλιος στό θυμητικό
νά γλυκολογᾶ, νά λιγοψυχᾶ
σάν τά χείλη ἀναστρέφονται
τά βλέφαρα συγκατανεύουν.

GEORGE SEFERIS

THREE SECRET POEMS

Upon a Ray of Winter Sun

1
Leaves of rusted tin
for the poor mind that has seen the end;
the scanty glimmerings.
Leaves that swirl about with seagulls
angry with the winter.

Like breasts bursting free
the dancers became trees
a large forest of naked trees.

2
The white seaweeds are burning
Old Women* emerging without eyelids
shapes that used to dance
flames that became marble.
Snow has covered the world.

3
My mates had maddened me
with theodolites sextants lodestones
and telescopes that enlarged things—
better they'd stayed away.
Where will such roads take us?
But this day which began
perhaps hasn't faded yet
with a fire in a ravine like a rose
and an airy sea by God's feet.

4
Years ago you said:
"Fundamentally I am a matter of light."

And even now when you lean
against the broad shoulders of sleep
even when they cast you
into the benumbed bosom of the open sea
you search into corners where the dark
is worn and can no longer hold
you seek gropingly for the spear
which is destined to pierce your heart
to open it to the light.

5
Which muddy river has carried us away?
We stayed at the bottom.
The current flows over our heads
bending the mute reeds;

the voices
beneath the chestnut tree have become pebbles
and the children are throwing them.

6
A short breath and another breath, a gust
as you leave the book
and tear useless papers from the past
or bend to see in the meadow
arrogant centaurs galloping
or unripe amazons sweating
in all their bodies' furrows
as they contest in jumping and wrestling.

Resurrectional gusts one dawn when
you thought the sun had come out.

7
Flame is healed by flame
not in the slow passing of time
but in a flash, all at once;
like a desire that merged with another

and both remained nailed down
or like
the rhythm of music that remains
there in the center like a statue

immovable.

This breath is not a passage
steering of thunder.

*The Graiae of Greek Mythology.

University of British Columbia *Contemporary Literature in Translation,* No. 9 (Winter, 1970), 5.

On Stage

1.
Sun, you're playing with me
but this is no dance
all this nakedness
almost blood
perhaps some wild forest;
then—

2.
Gongs were heard
and the messengers came;
I wasn't expecting them
even their voices were forgotten;
rested, just having dressed
holding baskets with fruit.
I marvelled and whispered:

"I like amphitheatres."
The shell filled at once
and the light dimmed on the stage
as if for a notorious murder scene.

3.
What were you seeking? with stammering looks.
You had hardly gotten up
leaving the sheets to freeze
and the baths of vengeance.
Drops rolling down your shoulders
your belly
your feet bare on the dirt
on the mown grass.
Those three,
the faces of bold Hekate,
were trying to take you with them.
Your eyes two tragic shells
and you had on the nipples of your breasts
two little purple pebbles—
stage props, I don't know.
They were shouting for joy
you remained rooted to the earth;
their gestures were tearing the air.
Slaves brought them the knives;
you remained rooted to the earth
a cypress.
They drew the knives out of the sheaths
and looked for a spot to strike you.
Only then did you cry:
"Let anyone who wishes come sleep with me,
aren't I the sea, after all?"

4.
The sea; how has the sea become like that?
I lingered many years in the mountains;
the glow-worms blinded me.

Now on this beach I am waiting for
a man to moor
a remnant, a raft.
But can the sea fester?
A dolphin tore it once
and once again
the tip of a seagull's wing.

Yet the wave was sweet
where I plunged and swam as a child
even when I was a youth
as I was searching for shapes in the pebbles,
seeking patterns
the Old Man of the Sea* spoke to me:
"I am your country;
perhaps I am no one
but I can become what you wish."

5.
Who's heard at high noon
the grinding of the knife on the whetstone?
Which horseman's come
with kindling and torch?
Everyone washes his hands
and cools them.
And who's disembowelled
the woman the infant the house?
There is no culprit, smoke.
Who's left
clattering hoofs on the cobblestones?
They've abolished their eyes; blind.
There are no longer any witnesses left, for anything.

6.
When are you going to speak again?
Our words are children of many people
They are sown and born like infants

ake root and are nourished on blood.
Like pine trees
they keep the form of the wind
when the wind's gone, isn't there
to do words
they preserve the form of man
and man's gone, isn't there.
Perhaps the stars are trying to speak
those that trod on all your nakedness one night
Cygnus Sagittarius Scorpio
perhaps those.
But where will you be the moment when
in this very theatre the light comes on?

7.

Yet there, on the other shore
under the black glance of the cave
suns in your eyes, birds on your shoulders
you were there; you were in pain because
of the other labor, the love
the other dawn, the presence
the other birth, the resurrection;
yet there you were coming into being again
in time's excessive dilation
moment by moment like resin
like a stalactite, a stalagmite.

Proteus of the Greek Mythology

Fairleigh Dickinson University *The Literary Review,* XVI, No. 3 (Spring, 1973), 295-298.

Summer Solstice

1
The greatest sun on one side
and the new moon on the other
distant in memory like those breasts.
Between them the chasm of the starry night
deluge of life.

The horses on the threshing-floors
gallop and sweat
upon scattered bodies.
All are going there
and that woman whom
you saw beautiful, in a moment
is bending, can endure no longer, has knelt.
The millstones are grinding them all
and all become stars.

Eve of the longest day.

2.
All have visions
yet no one will admit it;
They go thinking they're alone.
The large rose
had always been there
by your side deeply in sleep
yours and unknown.
But only now that your lips've touched it
on the outermost leaves
have you felt the dancer's dense weight
falling into the river of time—
the dreadful splash.
Don't waste the breath this respite
has granted you.

3.
But in this sleep
a dream so easily degenerates
into a nightmare.
Like the fish that glittered under the wave
and plunged into the slimy depth
or a chameleon when he changes color.
In the city that's become a brothel
panders and whores
peddle decayed delights;
the wave-borne girl
wears a cow's hide
for the bullock to mount her;
the poet
hoodlums throw filth at him
as he looks at the statues dripping blood.
You must get out of this sleep;
this flogged hide.

4.
In the mad wind-scattering
right and left up and down
sweepings're whirled about.
Thin deadly fumes
paralyze the limbs of people.
Souls
hurry to part from bodies
thirst and can find water nowhere;
they stick here and there at random
birds on lime-twigs;
fluttering in vain
till they can no longer lift their wings.

This place gets drier all the time
an earthen jar.

5.

The world wrapped in benumbing sheets
has nothing else to offer
but this end.
                    In the warm night
the withered priestess of Hekate
with naked breasts up on the terrace
is entreating an artificial fullmoon, while
the young servant girls yawn and
stir in a copper cauldron
aromatic potions.
Those who like perfumes tomorrow will have their fill.
Her passion and her make-up
are like those of the dramatic actress
their plaster has already peeled.

6.

Down there at the laurel trees
down there at the white oleanders
down there at the thorny rock
and the glassy sea at our feet.
Remember the tunic you were watching as it
opened and then slid slowly down over the nakedness
and fell around the ankles
dead—
if that sleep could fall so
among the laurels of the dead.

7.

The poplar in the small garden
its breath measures your hours
day and night;
an hour-glass filled by the sky.
With the power of the moon its leaves
drag black footsteps on the white wall.
The pines at the border are scant
then marble and a flood of light

and people as people are made.
But the blackbird twitters
when coming to have a drink
and you may even hear the voice of the turtle-dove.
In the small garden ten strides long
you can see the sunlight
fall on two red carnations
on an olive tree and some honeysuckle.

Accept who you are.

The poem
do not cast it into the deep plane trees
nourish it with the earth and rock you have.
As for more—
dig at the same place to find them.

8.
The blank page, a cruel mirror
reflects only what you used to be.

The blank page speaks in your voice,
your own voice
not the one you like;
your music is this life
you have wasted.
You can earn it back if you wish to
if you nail yourself on this indifferent object
that throws you back
to where you started from.

You've travelled, you've seen many a moon and sun
you've touched dead and living men
you've felt the young man's pain
and the woman's groan
and the unripe child's bitterness—
whatever you felt collapses in an empty heap
unless you trust this void.

You may find there what you'd thought lost;
the budding of youth, the just
                    submersion of old age.

Your life is what you've given
this void is what you've given,
the blank page.

9.
You were talking about things they couldn't see
and they were laughing.

But to row on the dark river
up stream;
to follow the ignored road
blindly, stubbornly
and to keep searching for deeply-rooted words
like the much-knotted olive tree—
let them laugh.
And to long for the other world also to dwell
in today's smothering solitude
in this ruined present—
leave them.

The sea wind and the freshness of dawn
exist though no one has asked that it be so.

10.
The hour when dreams come true
when sweetly breaks the day
I saw the lips opening
leaf by leaf.

A slim sickle shone in the sky.
I was afraid it might mow them down.

11.
The ocean they call calm
ships and white sails
a breeze from the pines and the mountain of Aegina
a panting breath;
your skin was slipping on her skin
easy and warm
a thought hardly made immediately forgotten.

But in the shallows
a harpooned octopus spurted ink
and at the bottom—
if you could imagine how far
                    the beautiful islands extend.
I was staring at you with all the light and darkness
                    I possess.

12.
The blood is now bursting
as the heat swells
in the veins of the festered sky.
It seeks to pass through death
to find joy.

The light is a pulse
continually slower and slower
you think it is about to stop.

13.
A little longer and the sun will stop.
The spirits of the dawn
blew in the dry conches;
the bird chirped three times
                    three times only;
the lizard on the bleached stone
remains motionless
looking at the scorched grass

where the snake slid.
A black wing draws a deep line
high in the blue dome—
look at it, it's about to open.

Resurrectional labor.

14.
Now,
with the molten lead of divination
the gleam of the summer sea,
the nakedness of a whole life;
and the passing by and the stopping and
                        the lying down and the tossing
the lips the caressed fleece,
all seek to be burnt.

Like the pinetree at high noon
possessed by its resin
is eager to give birth to flames
and can no longer bear the torture—

Call the children to collect the ash
and sow it.
Whatever happened, happened right.
And even whatever didn't happen
must also burn
this noon that the sun was nailed
to the heart of the centipetal rose.

Fairleigh Dickinson University *The Literary Review*, XVI,
No. 3 (Spring, 1973), 299-302.

Louisiana State University *The Southern Review*, V, No. 2
(Spring, 1969), 522-7.

University of British Columbia *PRISM International*, No. 3
(Spring, 1970), 102-3.

"Against Whitethorns . . ."

(The *Republic,* X, 616)

Sunium was beautiful on that Annunciation day
returning with the spring.
Sparse green leaves around the rusty rocks
red earth and whitethorns
showing their full-blown long needles and yellow blossoms.
Farther away ancient columns, a harp's strings can still
be heard . . .
Calm.
—What might've reminded me of that Ardiaeus?
A word in Plato, I think, one lost in my mind's channels;
the yellow shrub's name
hasn't changed since those times.
That evening I found the passage:
"They bound his hands and feet," it tells us
"they flung him down and flayed him,
dragged him aside and carded him
against the prickly whitethorns,
then they went and tossed him into Tartarus, a shredded rag."

This way in the underworld was paying for his crimes
Ardiaeus the Pamphylian, the most wretched Tyrant.

31 st of March, 1971

Louisiana State University, *The Southern Review,* IX, No. 3
(Summer, 1973), 680-681.

REVIEWS

REVIEWS

Reviewing a book of poetry in translation is a rather demanding and complicated professional process. Such a review must deal with a number of issues, problems, and details, and cover considerable ground in the realms of the two literatures involved, the original and that of the target tongue.

More specifically, in discussing the merits of an English translation of an anthology of Greek poems, or of a representative collection of a major poet's work, or even of his complete works, I suggest that the reviewer must take all or most of the following steps:

1. A brief but incisive presentation of the Greek poet must be made (with significant facts, events, dates) for the benefit of anglophone readers who know nothing, or next to nothing, about him and his times in Greece. In the case of an anthology a similar collective presentation must be made comprehensively covering the represented poets and their place in the history of their national literature.

2. The Greek poet and his work must be evaluated and classified on the basis of existing international artistic "schools," trends, and the like, and their degree of relationship to them must be made clear by means of references to comparisons and analogues. For instance, Solomos's romanticism, liberalism, and style may be compared to those of Byron, Shelley, and Manzoni. Sikelianos's lyricism, symbolism, and occultism may be discussed by analogy to those of W.B. Yeats.

3. After these general remarks, which create a necessary background for the appreciation of the text, we must briefly discuss the text that appears in translation, and explain its

artistic, thematic, and historical or cultural problems, peculiarities, and complexities.

4. We may then proceed with an examination of the accuracy and artistic quality of the translation itself. If it is accurate or not, aesthetically satisfactory or not, will have to be inferred from the number and nature of telling examples we will quote and analyze.

Some reviewers who do not know Greek, certainly bypass this step, and pretend that the question of accuracy and artistic success is answered by the prestige and authority of the translator, or of his academic position in a fine university. Since, however, unprofessional practices have been discovered, in relation to the translation of Greek verse by "big shots" in the broad anglophone world, a review that ignores the Greek language, and the translator's mastery of it, is unprofessional and unscholarly.

5. A short concluding statement will close the review. It may praise (or chastise) the translator, the publishers, and all those involved in the making and circulation of the books; it may even include hints about the need for more projects of that kind, or any information about related activities (research, translation, criticism) by other scholars in the field.

The above statement does not purport to be an absolute or unique formula. Excellent and more scholarly reviews have been published by more gifted or more scholarly specialists and academics. The reviews I have collected here were judged, and then published, by experts manning the editorial boards of a number of prestigious university presses. That is why I believe that a young learner, who desires to a do a professional review of this kind, will never go wrong if he begins by following these logical and simple steps. Eventually he may formulate his own, more personal, approach and strategy.

My reviews cover all of the most important English translations of major Greek poets in book form since the late 1960s. Cavafy, Palamas, Sikelianos, Seferis, Elytis, Ritsos, Sinopoulos, and those represented in anthologies or collections are presented in them. The reader will have to tolerate some inevitable repetitions of data, comments, characterizations, historical backgrounds, and examples in two or more reviews that discuss the same artist, or even the same work by the same artist (Palamas's 'Ο Δωδεκάλογος τοῦ Γύφτου, and its three different versions, for instance).

No reader, scholarly or naive, should jump to *oversimplified conclusions* about an artist's or a scholar's social philosophy or political ideology because I may have used the term 'Marxist' to explain his world view. Marxism should not always be equated to Russian Communism. Being a Marxist or a Communist does not necessarily mean that a person is an agent or a spy of the Soviet Union. Also, when I imply that an intellectual is, or is not, a Marxist or Communist, I am talking about that person's beliefs, not about *mine*. Finally, when I say that a poet was not a Marxist (or did not openly express political ideologies in his verse), that does not mean that he was an anti-Marxist, a fascist, a C.I.A. agent, or an idiot.

1

George Seferis: *Collected Poems 1924-1955*. Trans-
lated, Edited and Introduced by Edmund Keeley and
Philip Sherrard.
Princeton: Princeton University Press, 1967. 490 pp.

Other than Nikos Kazantzakis, George Seferis is undoubtedly the best-known literary figure of modern Greece.
Many of his poems had appeared in translation in a number of
European and American magazines since the 1930s and 1940s
respectively. The awarding of the Nobel Prize for Literature
in 1963 was preceded and followed by the publication, in
book form this time, of most of his easily translatable poems
in English, French, German, Italian, Spanish, Danish, and
Swedish. By "translatable" I refer to Seferis' poems written
mostly in free verse and not utilizing the stanzaic and stylistic
conventions of the rich poetic tradition of modern Greece.

The English-speaking public found access to the work of
Seferis mostly through Professor Rex Warner's thin volume
of translations, *Poems* (London, 1960; Boston, 1961; also
paperback). Though Warner's edition was received well the
need for a complete, and if possible, bilingual volume remained. Professor Edmund Keeley of Princeton and Mr.
Philip Sherrard of the British School of Archaeology in
Athens, aided by the Whitney Darrow Publication Reserve
Fund, have collaborated in translating, editing, and introducing this impressive bilingual volume.

Few scholars have done so much in translating and presenting critically modern Greek poetry and prose as these two
men and their group of Greek relatives and friends. The high
quality of their work is manifested in this book too. The
original has been transcribed correctly *en face* of the translation. A brief but incisive foreword helps the reader under-

stand Seferis' straddling position between the Greek and the Western poetic traditions. A selected bibliography, a list of explanatory notes, and biographical data complete this scholarly and almost luxurious edition.

Keeley and Sherrard are creative writers as well, and their ability for translating Greek free verse is of the highest order. What they achieve astonishingly well is rendering Seferis' Greek into a kind of English whose tone and flavor closely reflect the Seferian idiom and style. On the other hand, this English is equally acceptable to audiences on either side of the Atlantic. This is something that other translators of Seferis have not always achieved. For example, one of the lines of "In the Manner of G.S." is translated by Rex Warner, "I met old John. He stood me an ice." Keeley and Sherrard avoid the British idiom and translate, without changing the punctuation, in more general English, "I met Yiannı and he treated me to an ice cream." This line sounds as well in America as it does in England: moreover, it is more faithful to the Greek since it does not contain the adjective "old" which Warner had to add to "John" to make it correspond somehow to the familiar Greek "Yianni." On the other hand, the term and title "Myth of our History," suggested by Lawrence Durrell and G. Katsimbalis first and reiterated by Kimon Friar in 1953, is more successful than "Mythistorema," which may sound too Greek to those who are not capable of immediately discerning the words *myth* and *history* in it. Keeley and Sherrard, however, often seem to prefer to render a modern Greek name or term in its phonetic form rather than its English equivalent; they prefer "Syntagma," "Yianni," "Agonia," to Warner's "Constitution," "John," and "Agony." And, in my opinion, their versions sound more poetic than his, and of course communicate the Greekness of the poem more directly.

In his work Seferis shows a unique understanding of the cultural inheritance of the modern Greek intellectual. As a poet of Greece Seferis writes about himself, his people, and his land but not in a strictly national and ephemeral spirit. The characters or *personae* he presents (who seem to derive from classic, Byzantine, or contemporary Greek situations; or from French symbolists and surrealists; or from T. S. Eliot, Ezra Pound, and even Pirandello) remain exponents of issues and feelings which transcend the limits of Greece, or of Europe; and their messages reach Everyman—not just the Greek—everywhere and at any time.

The perennial significance of most of Seferis' themes can be best experienced in "The King of Asine," one of his greatest poems. With Olympian, and more specifically Apollonian, serenity and clarity the poem explores the meaning of the futility and brevity of human glory and existence. This theme is as old as the world. The Biblical authors (in *Ecclesiastes*), Shelley (in "Ozymandias"), François Villon (in *Le grand testament*), Victor Hugo (in *Les misérables*) have spoken, among many others, philosophically, nostalgically or bitterly about it. Seferis, however, succeeds in creating a powerful feeling of void, both personal as well as universal, by dramatically staging the "action" of the poem at the ancient ruins of Homeric Asine. At the edge of the rock, where the sea eternally touches the hanging vines and branches, the conscience of time loses its value: present and past fuse into one. Nothing in the area suggests anything about the King who one ruled here. A gold death mask in a museum may represent him or, indeed, any other ancient monarch. But this mask is empty and cold. Similarly, the dryness, ruins, and emptiness of the unchangeable landscape offer the poet an opportunity to examine the meaning of his own existence against this timeless background. The result is the same. The search for the forgotten King and for the *self* of the poet concludes with the realization that"Under the mask a void," and ". . . the poet a void." Seferis thus fuses the confessional with the universal element in the poem, and reaches his conclusion in a subtle and faultless way.

In a more recent poem, "Helen," inspired by Euripides' eponymous drama, Seferis expresses the feeling of the futility of war. At that time (early 1950s) he was Ambassador of

Greece in the Middle East and in this capacity he visited the troubled island of Cyprus repeatedly. One might expect the Greek poet to have written about the island in a nationalistic spirit. Yet Seferis, with the wisdom and worldliness of a professional diplomat, in this poem obviously deplores this conflict—indirectly—as he states the tragic futility of all wars. Thus, once again, he succeeds in fusing the personal with the universal as he concludes his reflections on the myth concerning the beautiful Helen of Troy. "On sea-kissed Cyprus,/consecrated to remind me of my country/I moored alone with this fable,/if it's true that it is a fable,/if it's true that mortals will not again take up/the old deceit of the gods;/if it's true/that in future years some other Teucer,/or some Ajax or Priam or Hecuba,/or someone unknown and nameless who nevertheless saw/a Scamander overflow with corpses,/isn't fated to hear/newsbearers coming to tell him/that so much suffering, so much life,/went into the abyss/all for an empty tunic, all for a Helen." In this version one also sees that the translators prefer the latinized form of classical Greek names, unlike, for instance, the classicist Richmond Lattimore who prefers transliterations of the originals (Teukros, Aias, Hekabe, Skamandros, etc.).

This edition is a must for the serious reader of modern poetry—not just the admirer of modern Greek culture. And it will remain the standard volume of Seferis for a few years. I say a few years for two main reasons. First, this *Collected Poems 1924-1955* was, it seems, not originally intended to be a volume of "collected" poems. As an afterthought the earlier and rhymed poems of Seferis were added, in an appendix, to the later collections in free verse. This almost arbitrary breaking of the chronological order mars an otherwise almost perfect work. The reader has to do research within it in order to follow the chronological development of the poems and the various phases which the poet went through before finding his "final" idiom and style. Thus, three of the rhyming poems of *Turning Point* (1931) have been omitted completely, and six from *Book of Exercises, Logbook I, Logbook II,* plus all of *The Cistern* have been taken out of their proper sequence and placed in the appendix. All of the appendix poems (some 20% of the whole) have been translated almost literally without any attempt at approximating the rhythm and rhyming pattern of the originals. This is a shame, because Seferis' early work is not that of a novice. With its half-rhymes, off-rhymes, ellipses and other devices, Seferis' early work acquires a certain aura and poetic quality reminiscent of Emily Dickinson's. A number of these poems have been set to music by competent composers (like Mikis Theodorakis), and at least one, "Denial," has become widely known all over Greece. The free-verse rendition of these conventionally structured, disciplined, and rhymed poems leaves much to be desired. Perhaps Keeley and Sherrard and their team ought to have invited the assistance of one of these poet-translators, in this country or overseas, who have demonstrated their ability to imitate or recreate the rhyme schemes and musical effects and various originals, without deviating substantially from the intended meaning and form. Richard Wilbur, Michael Hamburger, Barbara Gibbs, and even Robert Lowell are names that come easily to mind in this respect.

The second reason why this volume is destined to be superseded before too long comes from the fact that Mr. Seferis (born in 1900) is now retired from the diplomatic corps of Greece and has more free time than before. In 1966 he published a new collection consisting of three long sequences, *Three Secret Poems*. This thin volume has not been included in *Collected Poems 1924-1955*, though the translators mention it in their bibliography and a note. One can expect more poems to be written by Seferis in the next few years, and a "Complete Poems" will be in order. But for the time being the Keeley-Sherrard edition has met the need for a more complete and responsible presentation of Seferis' work and easily supersedes Rex Warner's pioneer effort.*

Kostes Palamas, *The King's Flute,* tr. with an Introduction by Frederic Will.
Lincoln: University of Nebraska Press, 1967, xxxviii +
226 pp.

Kostes Palamas, *The Twelve Words of the Gypsy,* tr.
with an Introduction by Frederic Will.
Lincoln: University of Nebraska Press, 1964, xxi+205pp.

Kostes Palamas (1859-1943) remains one of modern
Greece's most popular and respected poets. The title of
National Poet (or Laureate) was deservedly given to him, and
several critics have tried to make his work known outside the
narrow confines of Greece. But Palamas' poetry has ob-
stinately refused to yield to the determined efforts of many
translators into English, French, and other languages. The
reasons for this failure are quite simple, for Palamas has
created a highly poetic language which draws on elements
from Homeric or Byzantine Greek, from peasant dialects
and formal expressions, from folk song and contemporary
Athenian idiom. The style of Palamas, especially in his longer
compositions, is often rhetorical and even verbose. He likes
compound words and makes up his own adjectives, which he
piles up on nouns with a skill reminiscent of Homer's. His
subject-matter and imagery usually derive from the inexhaustible cultural tradition of classical Hellas, Byzantium,
and modern Greece. Accordingly the non-Greek readers who
are capable of appreciating him are mostly Byzantinologists
and historians. The numerous volumes of verse written by
Palamas exhibit his ability to compose couplets, quatrains,
sonnets, verse dramas, poems in rhyming and unrhyming
fifteen-syllable lines, a variety of other conventional stanzaic
forms and meters, and even free verse.

It is not surprising, then, that no translator thus far has been able to successfully render Palamas' verse into another language. The Greek historical, cultural, and linguistic tradition ominously looms on the translator's horizon. Attempts, however, have been made. Some simply translated Palamas into prose. But Palamas—though a serious and, at times, rather profound writer—was neither a systematic philosopher nor an original sage. He was a lyrical poet, and his thoughts and feelings become great poetry only when expressed via a richly adorned, musical, impressive and connotative diction. The simple prose or prosaic translations of this kind of poetry by admirers of the poet (Eugène Clèment in France; A. Phoutrides, D. Michalaros, R. Dalvin and others in this country) have failed to convince readers that Palamas is a poet, let alone a great poet.

The same is, unfortunately, true of the translations made by Frederic Will. Professor Will, who readily admits that he is not a Neo-Hellenic scholar and uses Clèment's French prose version as a kind of "control," must be commended for his will and courage in translating the more than eight thousand lines of Palamas' lyrical epics *The Twelve Words of the Gypsy* (1907) and *The King's Flute* (1910). Mr. Will provides interesting introductions to both volumes and discusses style, plots, themes, structure, and historical background adquately. But the poetic flavor and amazing diction of Palamas —let alone his fast flowing rhythms and melody—have rarely been caught in this version. Thus *The Twelve Words* (Cantos) *of the Gypsy*—in which Palamas utilized an impressive variety of stanzaic and rhyming patterns, internal rhymes, ellipses, and other late Victorian technical devices—has been rendered into prosaic free verse. For instance, Mr. Will's stanza "I with no theologies/who bend not to any gods—/you are my fidelity and truth!/I took the churches one by one" (p. 41), in the original is a very musical quatrain rhyming a, b, c, b; with seven to eight syllables per line; with four stresses on alternate lines (1 and 3), and three stresses on the others (2 and 4).

The popular *dekapentasyllabos* (a fifteen-syllable line, very common in modern Greek balladry or sophisticated verse, the closest equivalent to the English blank verse) with occasional rhymes of *The King's Flute* has been rendered into a much greater number of lines of equally stiff free verse. For example, the four-line passage "Who is the son of the widow, who, the/musknursed prince,/desire of an entire people, idol;/and if Kroutagos holds him, what evil will follow?" is Mr. Will's version of just three perfectly metered and accented musical fifteen-syllable lines of the Greek.

Mr. Will persuasively argues about the tremendous difficulties involved in the translation of these two Neo-Hellenic literary monuments, but he also admits that he has willfully overlooked much good advice. When one considers, however, that Kimon Friar succeeded in translating 33,333 Greek seventeen-syllable lines into the same number of English consistently metered and accented lines throughout Kazantzakis' *Odyssey,* then Mr. Will's arguments lose much of their strength. If these two long translations were literally correct, the two volumes could at least be read by readers who are interested and curious to see what this poet had to say about Gypsies, Kings, and Flutes.

In *The Twelve Words of the Gypsy,* Palamas presents the Gypsy as the individuated representative of his race, and as a dynamic symbol of restlessness and freedom from tradition and responsibility. This *persona,* then, in some respects is not unlike the Greek; both value their individuality and race more than anything else. But this manly attitude has ominous implications for the cosmopolitan and multiracial Empire of Constantinople. The Emperor, in his pursuit of pleasure, is indifferent to the steady rise of the Turks (c. 1350 A.D.). The Gypsy experiences the two forms of Hellenism—pagan and Christian—and senses their eventual fusion into one. Thus he prophesies death and a future resurrection. In this particular function the poet seems to identify and merge with the *persona* he has created.

All this and much more is synthesized by Palamas' compelling imagination into a kind of artistic expression (by means of lyrical philosophizing) of his anxiety *vis à vis* the historical reality and destiny of modern Greece.

By contrast *The King's Flute,* a story within a story, is less vague and fuzzy, and seems bound to historical detail. Its hero is the Emperor Basil II (957-1025) who travels accompanied by his army, from Constantinople through Greece to Athens on a pilgrimage to worship the Virgin Mary in the Parthenon, which had been converted to a Christian Cathedral. The nature of this epic is more narrative than philosophical. Basil's journey constitutes a symbolic tribute to the unbroken unity of Hellenism. Athene and her Parthenon are continued, or transformed, into Mary and the Church Byzantium with its splendor and culture is, it seems, the historical and physical continuation and development of classical Hellas. And contemporary Greece is—the nationalist poet implies—just another link in this chain of glorious tradition, despite all its recent misfortunes and hardships.

These two lyrical epics should be considered companion pieces. The first is concerned with feelings and thoughts aroused by the inevitable loss of worldly empire and glory. The second helps the poet (and the Greek reader) to recover from the impact of that loss through an examination of the great past and the recognition of Hellenism's dynamic and uninterrupted historical continuity.

A general idea of Palamas' achievement can de derived from these two translations. But the texts are studded with numerous and unwarranted deviations from the exact expression of the poet, and not a few mistakes in meaning. Some of these alterations might be excused if the translator had attempted a faithful imitation of style, meter, form, and rhyme. But since Mr. Will did not do that—and did not have to change words and diction in order to "force" the original meter or rhyme into English—most of his changes are arbitrary and unfortunate. For instance, in *The Twelve Words of the Gypsy,*

185

"Word Five" Palamas writes, "it is as if they are waiting for expensive cargoes." Mr. Will changes adjective and verb, "it is as if they carry/priceless cargoes" (p. 54). In "Word Seven" the adjective *harokopa* (fun-loving, gay and unthoughtful) becomes "lovely" (p. 89); its plural, however, is rendered in another line as "hedonists" (p. 114). The noun to *planema* (wandering here and there) becomes "course" (p. .89). In "Word Eight" *ton parastratemenon* (the wayward; those who went astray) is translated literally as "men who lost the way" (p. 114). Further down the translator has "whores" (p. 126) where Palamas has written *pornovoskoi* (pimps, panders).

In *The King's Flute,* errors are more abundant. In "Prologue" Palamas writes, "Extinguished all creative fires in the land." The translator alters it to "Darkened all creative lights in the land" (p. 1), thus eliminating the connotation of fire as creative passion or inspiration (cf. Prometheus). On page 2 he abides by this translation, but on page 3 the same Greek phrase is correctly rendered as "creative flames." Palamas continues, "Everywhere, in the castle, in the heart, embers and ashes." Mr. Will extends for no apparent reason this one line into two and a half lines: "Everywhere/in the castle and in the heart,/half burnt fragments, ashes." The translation of the "Third Word" begins awkwardly, to say the least: "Triple streets, and quadruple streets, and paths" (p. 52). If one turns to the original, it can be seen that Palamas is referring to crossroads of various kinds by *tristrata kai tetrastrata.* In the beginning of the "Tenth Word" Palamas' Greek *to vios* (property, possessions) is rendered as "strength" (p. 184). The poet concludes his epic by referring to what happened to "the musical Flute," which the translator generously calls "the flute of the Muses" (p. 224). And so on. These are only instances picked at random.

In conclusion, one must stress the fact that George Seferis found his capable translators in the persons of Edmund Keeley, Philip Sherrard, and others; Nikos Kazantzakis spoke to us forcefully through Kimon Friar; but despite his good intentions and efforts, Mr. Will's Kostes Palamas remains an obscure and dull poet. Mr. Will's contribution to modern Greek letters, however, should not be judged solely on the basis of the scholarly and artistic success or failure of his Palamas versions. With this pioneer effort, he has actually cut a trail into the virgin territory called Palamas' lyrical epics. Now it is up to better equipped scholars and bards to follow the trail and do this great poet justice.* *

*Ohio University, *Mundus Artium,* I (Summer, 1968), No. 3, 103-106.
* *Indiana University, *Yearbook of Comparative and General Literature,* No. 18 (1969), 86-89.

3

Kostis Palamas, *The Twelve Lays of the Gypsy,* Translated, with an Introduction by George Thomson. London: Lawrence & Wishart, 1969. Pp. 146.

No poet of Modern Greece enjoyed the reputation and national acclaim that Kostis Palamas(1859-1943) did in his long poetic career. Several well-meaning translators and scholars have tried to make his work known outside the narrow confines of Greece. Unfortunately, Palamas' poetry has not yielded fully to any translator yet, and the French prose version of E. Clément, as well as the verse versions of A. Phoutrides, D. Michalaros, R. Dalvin, F. Will, and others in this country, have failed to convince poetry lovers that Palamas is the great poet that the Greeks claim him to be.

In his numerous volumes of verse, fiction, poetic drama, and literary criticism Palamas revealed his ability to draw plot material, imagery, and diction from the rich cultural tradition of classical Hellas, Byzantium, and Modern Greece —the three main phases of Hellenism which he always viewed as a dynamic, but essentially unified, cultural and historical phenomenon. Few poets ever succeeded, as he did, in enriching the demotic Greek (vernacular) with terms deriving directly from ancient or medieval Greek, from peasant dialects or contemporary Athenian idiom and descriptive adjectives, very often compound ones—the despair of all translators—which Palamas used with astonishing skill and frequency in emulation of the Homeric practice.

Because of the abundance of allusions to Greek history, folklore, and culture of all times, Palamas' poetry has been particularly attractive to classicists, historians, and Byzantinologists; whereas literary scholars do not seem to be aware of its existence.

Palamas' versatility as a poet can be seen in the amazing range of diction and musicality of his couplets, quatrains, sonnets, fifteen-syllable lines, a great variety of other conventional stanzaic forms and meters, and even high quality free verse. His reputation, however, as a profound poet and thinker rests mainly on lengthy compositions, fusing the lyric and epic genres and forms, such as ᾿Ασκραῖος (Askraios), ῾Ο Δωδεκάλογος τοῦ Γύφτου (The Twelve Cantos of the Gypsy), and ῾Η φλογέρα τοῦ Βασιλιᾶ (The King's Flute).

The greatest of all is *The Twelve Lays of the Gypsy* (as the British translator renders and spells it) which was completed by 1899 and published in 1907. In this "lyrical epic" (Palamas' own term) the poet used the *persona* of the Gypsy as the individuated representative of his nomadic race, as a dynamic symbol of restlessness and freedom from tradition and responsibility, who possesses the gifts of prophetic ability and objectivity. This hero then is much like the individualistic and, at times, Dionysian Greek. His pronounced individuality has ominous implications for the now diminished Byzantine Empire and the rising Turkish menace (c. 1350 A.D.). The Emperor, in his hedonistic pursuits, is indifferent to the danger that looms on the horizon. The Gypsy then experiences the two forms of Hellenism—classical and Christian—at their meeting point in history, and senses their eventual trials, the end of their present phase, and their inevitable fusion into one. Thus the Gypsy, like an Old Testament Prophet, foresees death as well as rebirth. In this particular function the poet seems to identify and merge with the *persona* he has created. The poem is actually Palamas' national prophecy and cultural legacy to his nation.

The composition of the poem was roughly contemporary with a national disaster. Greece had been humiliated in a foolhardy attempt to regain Greek territory from Turkey (1897) and become again an important power, an heir to

Byzantium—the obsession known as "the Great Idea." In his *Twelve Lays of the Gypsy* Palamas, acting instinctively as the Poet of his Nation, expressed his views and feelings *vis-à-vis* Modern Greece's obscure present and the great historical past of Hellenism. Rather than bemoan the actual conditions he prophesied, by means of the objective and detached Gypsy, that a brighter future was in store for Hellenism, though not in its immediate future, nor in the contemporary form.

This idea is reiterated and amplified in *The King's Flute* (1910), another lyrical epic, in which Palamas concentrated again on the time and place where the two main phases of Hellenism—one symbolized by Athena and the Parthenon, the glory that *was* Hellas; and the other by the Byzantine Emperor Basil II (957-1025) and the Christian Church, the glory that was the *New* Hellas—symbolically meet in Athens, and merge, so to speak, into one as their rôles and functions correspond; these are now expressed through new forms of worship, historical details, and sense of mission. This concept of historical-spiritual correspondence emphasizes Hellenism as a cultural continuum, a living inheritance.

These two poems, Palamas' masterpieces, are then companion pieces. The first is concerned with observations, and fears, provoked by the historical loss of empire and wordly glory. The second poem assists the poet, and the Greek intelligentsia, in recovering from the dejection caused by this sense of loss through an *excursus* into the greatness of the Greek past, and the discovery and recognition that the past actually lives in the present, and that Hellenism is a dynamic and uninterrupted spiritual entity which changes forms but never ceases to be.

In *The Twelve Lays of the Gypsy* the reader experiences descriptive narrative, meditative, and quasi-philosophical passages, as well as verbose rhetoric and lines of exquisite lyricism. Since atmosphere, tone, and purpose vary from lay to lay, Palamas employs a wide range of verse forms and meter schemes in order to express his ideas in the most suitable poetic form. Only a virtuoso translation of high quality could possibly approximate, if not match, what Palamas achieved through his Greek.

Professor George Thomson, an eminent classicist and prolific author, knows his Modern Greek and generally translates words and idioms with relative accuracy and skill. He does, however, rather often omit, add, or change words here and there in the poem with the freedom of an enthusiastic philologist engaged in the textual emendation of a poorly preserved papyrus. For instance, he adds the words "two," "No," "memories," and "madcap" to his text (pp. 43, 44, 83 and 105 respectively); he omits the words "belligerent," "enslaved," and "monks" (pp. 44, 83 and 84); he changes the adjective ἐρωτόπαθη (amorous) to "mad passion," χρόνων (of years, of time) to "history," and λυχνιτάρια (isinglass, mica) to "rubies" (all on p. 43). Similarly τεράστιος (huge) becomes "terrible" (p. 46); persons of pronouns are often changed for no apparent reason, "you" becomes "they" (p. 44), and "my" is rendered in the third person (p. 105) . . . Τρούλους . . . σαράγια (domes and seraglios) is translated as "pinnacles and cupolas" (p. 44). And so on. These are only random observations.

A charitable critic, I suppose, may accept most of these liberties as peccadillos, or even as matters of taste. The fact is, however, that the translator does not commit all these minor sins out of necessity, but by choice, and one has to disagree with his choice. If Mr. Thomson were translating Palamas with an eye on form, meter, rhythm, and rhyme-scheme one might say that some changes would be necessary and justified in order to transpose the whole poem—not only its meaning—into English. But there is where his inability to translate the poem as a poem is, unfortunately, evidenced. Not a single stanza form, pattern of rhyme, or metrical scheme has been approximated, let alone imitated. Even the form of the poem has been flagrantly violated, and its length reduced at least by one third.

The last lay (or canto), "To a Woman," in the original consists of fifty-seven rhyming couplets (114 lines) of fifteen syllables each. Mr. Thomson turns it into fifty-nine single, extremely long, prosaic lines, with no meter or rhyme. The prosaic "With no struggle, not even a stifled cry, there unfolds a drama in my soul./Your strong hands gird me round, yet I am the dank night which cannot be enclosed" (p. 142), is what Mr. Thomson made of these two melodious couplets:

Χωρίς κανένα ἀγώνα, κανένα σκοῦσμα, ὢϊμέ!
πλέκεται κάποιο δρᾶμα μέσ᾽ στήν ψυχή μου ἐμέ.

Τά δυνατά σου χέρια γιά ζώνη μοῦ περνᾶς·
τἄζωστο ξάπλωμα εἶμαι μιᾶς νοτερῆς νυχτιᾶς.

The octets of Lay XII, with alternating rhymes and half-rhymes, with eight to eleven syllables per line, have become free verse quatrains. Palamas' quatrains in Lays III, IV, VII, IX, X, and XI (usually rhyming abab or abca) are squeezed by Mr. Thomson into long, run-on, prosaic paragraphs, unrhyming, and arranged to look like free verse. Palamas' few quintets and sestets in the poem share a similar fate—reduction to a smaller number of prose lines, occasionally sounding like free verse. This metamorphosis of the poem in terms of form, style, and rhythm is, to say the least, unfortunate. Despite the translator's adherence to the meaning of the work as a document, a poem is a poem, and should remain a poem in its translation.

Also, instead of transliterating Greek names, as is now the practice (cf. translations of Greek texts by Richmond Lattimore, Robert Fitzgerald, Albert Cook, *et al.*), Mr. Thomson still uses the Latinized spelling, following "the traditional way," or a kind of phonetic spelling of Modern Greek names (p. 143). The result is, of course, errors and confusion. The Spartan river Eurotas becomes "Evrotas," Nikephoros becomes "Nikiforos," and Hymettos changes to "Hymettus," but Lykos and Pentadaktylon are simplified to "Likos" and "Pendadaktilon," whereas Olympos and Orpheus are both made to end, erroneously for one of them, in -us.

Last but not least, Professor Thomson must be approached with skepticism in his otherwise scholarly and informative introduction. The brief chapters which try to play up Marxist undertones and themes in *The Twelve Lays of the Gypsy,* a poem written before the turn of the century in Greece, are clearly misleading. Praise for laborers and disdain for effete snobs are shared equally by both leftist internationalists and chauvinistic Greek nationalists (cf. today's ruling Junta) and the bourgeoisie in general. As for the demotic language of Palamas, Greece's dictator Gen. John Metaxas (1936-41) often used it in his speeches and broadcasts to the nation, as did many conservative writers.

The Gypsy has strong cultural and folkloric connotations for the Greek: he is fanatically individualistic, passionate, has survived racially against great odds, has prophetic powers, and though practically homeless, he can claim almost the whole world as his home. Rather than attempting—as the translator suggests—to undermine the social system of Greece after the defeat of 1897, Palamas was trying to console and encourage his countrymen with visions of hope.

If one examines Palamas' life and works as a whole, it must be noted that he enjoyed the honors, prizes, and positions that the conservative Greek establishment and the bourgeoisie generously bestowed on him (he was Secretary General of the University of Athens for decades, though he had never earned a degree, and the Government appointed him to the Academy when it was established in 1926). Throughout his poems nationalist intellectuals and even chauvinists found a plethora of ideas and facts consistent with their own beliefs. Greece's foremost conservative intellectuals and statesmen, Dr. Constantine Tsatsos, Dr. P. Kanellopoulos, as well as the leading literary critics, Mr. Emil Hourmouzios and Mr. I. M. Panayotopoulos, to name just two, have all written excellent lengthy monographs or scholarly essays on Palamas, in whose work they found nothing incompatible with their own socio-political ideology—by contrast to Mr. Thomson and his Marxist publishers.[1] Moreover, the Greek intellectual establishment, often aided by the Church, has always fought vehemently against writers whose leftist, Marxist, pacifist, or simply humanistic views were considered dangerous to the status quo. Palamas, however, never suffered the abuses that Kazantzakis, Ritsos, Vrettakos, Varnalis, and recently even Seferis and others did and still do.

If one compares or contrasts the British translation to the American one by Professor Frederic Will,[2] he must, undoubtedly, praise the former for the exact term "lay," for its greater accuracy, its introductory material the summaries of the lays, the addition of Palamas' own Preface, and the careful rendering and documentation of the epigraphs to each of the lays. On the other hand, the American version, despite its shortcomings, constitutes a more honest attempt to follow the form and the structural-stylistic mannerisms of the Greek text. As a matter of fact, Mr. Will is more accurate when he translates ʿΟ ἐρχομός as "The Coming," which Mr. Thomson turned into "The Arrival"—φτάσιμο or ἄφιξις in Greek. Also, Mr. Will's title "The Legend of the Tearless One" sounds more Greek and less British that "The Tale of Sir Tearless," of Mr. Thomson, which might remind one of Chaucer's lighter verse.

A careful reader will perceive the total image and symbolism of the Gypsy as he reads Mr. Thomson's Palamas. If, however, he wants to enjoy the *poetry* of Palamas' masterpiece, the reader will have either to learn Modern Greek or wait for a new translation.Professor Will cut a new trail of sorts with his pioneer work on Palamas' lyrical epics. Professor Thomson, who knew and disliked the American version, improved it only philologically. But as a *poem* Palamas' ʿΟ Δωδεκάλογος τοῦ Γύφτου has remained untranslated, and is still awaiting the real scholar-poet who can render it full artistic justice.

[1]Professor Thomson may have been influenced by the view of Kostas Varnalis and even Nikos Zachariades' book Ὁ ἀλη-θινός Παλαμᾶς (The Real Palamas). Both were avowed Marxists.

[2]For detailed reviews of Professor Will's Palamas translations see: *Greek Orthodox Theological Review,* XII (Winter 1966-67), 208-12; *Balkan Studies,* VII (1968), 214-15; *Yearbook of Comparative and General Literature,* No. 18 (1969), pp. 86-89.

University of Iowa, *Philological Quarterly,* XLIX, No. 2 (April, 1970), 278-282.

4

Kostes Palamas, *The Twelve Words of the Gypsy,* Translated by Theodore Ph. Stephanides and George C. Katsimbalis.
London, 1974, p. 194. Printed in Athens by F. Constantinidis & C. Michalas, Panepistimiou 39.

Though more than thirty years have passed since Kostes Palamas's death in 1943, and though most of his verse today sounds dated by contemporary aesthetic standards and philosophical trends, there are few literary historians and critics in Greece proper who will readily admit that his achievement and reputation as a poet of the Greek nation have been surpassed, or even equalled, by others so far in Greece.

This claim may surprise friends of modern Greek poetry in the English-speaking world, where the names of Constantine Cavafy, Nikos Kazantzakis, and George Seferis are well-known, and their works widely accepted as the greatest exemplars of the modern Greek Muse. This phenomenon is due, primarily, to two reasons. First, the very nature and quantity—not quality—of Palamas's verse; second the poor quality of the earlier English translations of his works, that is before the publication of the present volume.

Kazantzakis was fortunate to have found a poet-translator of the calibre and dexterity of Kimon Friar, whose masterful rendition of *The Odyssey: A Modern Sequel* (1958) made Kazantzakis's fame as a Greek poet known to dozens of thousands of English-speaking readers. Similarly, the brilliant work of Edmund Keeley, Philip Sherrard, George Savidis, and Walter Kaiser— plus a few others—succeeded in literally popularizing in international poetry circles Cavafy's eccentric verse and Seferis's esoteric lyricism, as their fine translations easily superseded earlier and rather inadequate versions of their poetry by others—with the exception of Kimon Friar's.

Until 1974 Palamas, unfortunately, had not fared well in this respect, and although the Greeks had stongly supported his candidacy for the Nobel Prize twice, his fame failed to spread beyond the rather narrow confines of Greece. Harvard classicist Aristides Phoutrides published the first book-length translations of Palamas's works into English: *Life Immovable* ('Ασάλευτη Ζωή), *A Hundred Voices* ('Εκατό Φωνές), and *Royal Blossom* (Τρισεύγενη), in verse, plus the short story *A Man's Death* (Θάνατος Παλληκαριοῦ) in 1919, 1921, 1923, and 1934 respectively[1]. Phoutrides's honest translations, however, are too literal, thus colorless and stilted. The late publisher of Chicago's *Athene,* Demetrios A. Michalaros, published in 1930 his metrical version of *The Grave* ('Ο Τά-φος)· but his good work went almost unnoticed, as did a few more scattered attempts by others.

During the last decaded, two more classicists, Professor Frederic Will in the United States, and Professor George Thomson in England, attempted to generate interest in Palamas by translating, separately, his two great lyrical epics: 'Ο Δωδεκάλογος τοῦ Γύφτου and ἡ Φλογέρα τοῦ Βασιλιᾶ. The first was attempted by both scholars, the second by Dr. Will only[2]. Much has been written about Will's and Thomson's translations by reviewers, including myself, the scholarly consensus being that their ambitious efforts resulted in utterly unpoetic, prosaic, and, in the case of Dr. Will, grossly inaccurate mistranslations. In effect, these two major poems had remained untranslated.

All these books, plus a few more lyrics translated by Rae Dalven and others, represent roughly one-fifth of Palamas's total output as poet, prose writer, and critic. Thus, quantitatively speaking, only a small fraction of this prolific author's astonishing contribution to modern Greek letters has been made available in English, and that in unsatisfactory translations mostly. By contrast, Cavafy's and Seferis's complete poetical works have appeared in fine English translations; and the bulk alone of Kazantzakis's colossal epic, plus the translations of most of his novels and several of his plays, constitute a rather impressive literary corpus for the English readership of modern Greek literature.

Up to now Palamas's poetry has steadfastly refused to yield to English translators. His highly lyrical language, enriched with elements from folk-song diction, contemporary sophisticated idiom, Byzantine, Hellenistic, and even classical Greek verbal expressions, plus his Homer-like fashioning of numerous compound adjectives and nouns (cf. περδικόστη-θη, ἐρωτόπαθη, νυχτοφέρνοντας), had created unsurmountable obstacles to all manner of well-meaning traslators. His subject-matter, imagery, allusions, and references—largely deriving from the long and inexhaustible cultural tradition and history of contemporary Greece, Byzantium, and ancient Hellas—similarly had posed tremendous problems of transposition to translators who acted only as linguistic interpreters.

In his subjective epic *The Twelve Words of the Gypsy,* first published in 1907, Palamas presents his nomadic hero as the individuated representative of his race, and as a dynamic symbol of human restlessness and freedom from responsibility and tradition. As he explains in his «Preface», Palamas identifies with the *persona* of the Gypsy, and at times he, the narrator's own voice, and the poet's identity seem to merge into, one consciousness—the Gypsy's. This Dionysian character owes much of his conceptualization to Palamas's knowledge of Nietzsche's theory of the Superman, as decades later Kazantzakis's own colorful Zorbas was to become an exponent—in part at least—of similarly Nietzschean influences. Both characters, however, despite their pronounced «internationalism», are in many respects typically Greek or Greek-like,· both valuing their freedom and individuality above anything else. In the poem, this romantic attitude of the Gypsy has ominous implications for the declining cosmopolitan Greek Empire of Constantinople. The pleasure-seeking Emperor, complacent in his pursuit of self-gratification, remains indifferent to the steady rise of the Turks (c. 1350). The Gypsy experiences the two seemingly antithetical

198

forms of Hellenism—pagan and Christian—and senses their eventual fusion into one, into a new culture combining elements from both. Thus Palamas, through his exotic mouthpiece, does not hesitate to prophesy death as well as a future resurrection. In this particular respect the poet symbolically accounts for the historical rise and fall of Hellenism, for the contemporary adversities of his nation (the 1897 defeat), and the inevitable racial survival of Hellenism in a new phase and form.

All these and much more are synthesized by Palamas's compelling imagination into a kind of artistic expression—by means of lyrical philosophising—of his anxiety *vis-à-vis* the historical reality and destiny of modern Greece. There is no doubt that Palamas succeeded in becoming the poetic spokesman of his nation's complex cultural consciousness and awareness, perhaps much more effectively that Tennyson, Longfellow, and Whitman ever became in their times and cultures.

Palamas's proverbial virtuosity in versification is triumphantly manifested in the numerous purple passages, varied stanzaic forms, rhyme schemes, and even free verse that he utilized in the composition of *The Twelve Words of the Gypsy*. Often rhetorical, and at times even verbose, his lines flow spontaneously and smoothly, always creating and maintaining melodious effects, as moods and tones shift, and rhythmic patterns change in endless succession.

It is exactly this astonishing, though traditional and conventional, skill in Palamas's art that had proven to be the Lydian stone in the translations of professors Will, Thomson, Phoutrides, Dalven and others. It is exactly in that area—successful transposition of rhythms, measures, poetic form and feeling—that the latest translators, Dr. Stephanides and Mr. Katsimbalis, have proven their skill and worth. To translate Palamas's verse one has to be a poet in his own right, plus, of course, quite an expert in modern Greek language, literature, and culture.

Stephanides and Katsimbalis are not novices in the field of English translation of Palamas poetry. Prior to the publication of their present book, they had published together two pamphlets with Palamas lyrics in their metrical versions: *Poems* (London, 1925), and *Three Poems* (London, 1969). These good translations, however, received little attention by comparatists and other literary scholars, mostly because they were published privately, and thus their promotion was quite limited. Stephanides, who is a retired London physician with several books of good English lyrics to his credit, and Katsimbalis, the famous *Colossus of Maroussi* of Henry Miller, and prolific writer, critic, editor, and reviewer in Athens for almost half a century, have now completed their English version of the *Ascraeus* too, which, we would like to hope, should be published sooner than other Palamas texts.

A comparison of random passages of the Stephanides-Katsimbalis translation of *The Twelve Words of the Gypsy*— as they have rendered the Greek word *logos*: canto, lay; plus the New Testament connotation—to those of others, reveals their strong poetic feeling and impressive ability to transpose Palamas's poem as a poem in English, not merely as a text, or literary document of sorts. Palamas opens his poem with the stanza:

> Τ' ἀξεδιάλυτα σκοτάδια
> τά χαράζει μιά λιγνή λευκότη
> νυχτοφέρνοντας καί αὐτή·
> καί εἴτανε τοῦ νοῦ μου ἡ πρώτη
> χαραυγή.
>
> (᾿Αθῆναι: Μπίρης, σελ. 303)

G. Thomson's prosaic version reduces the quintet to ... three rhymeless lines, thus violating its poetic substance and form:

> A faint glimness marks the impenetrable darkness
> Still full of night,
> It was my mind's first dawn.   (p. 43)

F. Will's slightly more artistic rendition mistranslates the word ἀξεδιάλυτα, among other weaknesses:

> Indissoluble shadows
> one thin light invades them
> swaddled itself in night;
> it was my mind's first
> dawn.   (p. 1)

Now, this is how Stephanides and Katsimbalis skillfully and creatively restore the poetic element of the original, without having to resort to free adaptation, «imitation» à la Robert Lowell, or *anaplasis:*

> Through the interwoven shadows
> Crept an evanescent gleam
> Mingled still with night;
> And it was my mind's own dawning
> Of the light.   (p. 25)

Also, here is their version of the famous Palamas quatrain in the beginning of Word III. Notice how well Katsimbalis and Stephanides have captured the rhythm and harmony of the Greek:

> Περδικόστηθη Τσιγγάνα
> ὦ μαγεύτρα, πού μιλεῖς
> τά μεσάνυχτα πρός τ᾽ ἄστρα
> γλῶσσα προσταγῆς,   (σελ. 329)

> Partridge-breasted Gypsy woman
> O enchantress! You who stand
> Speaking with the stars of midnight
> In a language of command,   (p. 55)

The above rendition virtually eclipses the following unpoetic and awkward ones by the two classisists:

Partridge-breasted gypsy,
magician, you who speak
at midnight to the stars
the commandements of the tongue,   (F. Will, p. 36)

and

O Gypsy woman, full-breasted as a partridge,
You witch, who speak a language of command
                                          (G. Thomson, p. 61)

Equal skill is exhibited by Katsimbalis and Stephanides in their rendering of rhyming couplets, ottava rimas, sestets, free verse etc. For instance, the epigrammatic couplet in the beginning of the Final Word, «To A Woman»:

Τά δυνατά σου χέρια τ᾽ ἄξια, τά κοσμικά,
χάρισμα πιό μεγάλο κι ἀπ᾽ τά φτερά.   (σελ. 445)

Your hands so strong and deft at homely things
Are gifts more precious than a pair of wings.   (p. 185)

Thomson arbitrarily twisted and compressed this couplet into . . . one long and pedestrian line of many syllabes: «Your strong, capable, skilled hands are a gift greater that wings;» (p. 141). And F. Will in vain arranged his prose to look like a couplet:

Your wordly, worthy, doing hands,
a gracing greater that from wings.   (p. 196)

Dr. Theodore Stephanides and Mr. George Katsimbalis wrote no introduction of their own, and let Kostes Palamas himself address his readers by means of his eloquent «Preface». They provided, however, a four-page «Glossary and Notes», plus a brief but precise «Analysis of the Poem» (pp. 21-24).

Let us hope that this excellent English translation of *The Twelve Words of the Gypsy* (1974) will help restore Palamas's reputation as a great visionary poet of modern Greece, and will persuade a serious academic press to present his beautiful and sonorous poetry to the English-speaking world.

Supplement: The above translation appeared one year later in a beautiful hardbound volume, with the Greek original *en face* of the English text: Kostes Palamas, *The Twelve Words of the Gypsy;* Translated by Theodore Ph. Stephanides and George C. Katsimbalis. Memphis State University Press, 1975. 314 pages.

[1]Kostes Palamas, *Life Immovable, First Part.* Translated by Aristides E. Phoutrides. Cambridge: Harvard University Press, 1919. *A Hundred Voices, and Other Poems, From the Second Part of "Life Immovable".* Translated with an Introduction and Notes by Aristides E. Phoutrides. Cambridge: Harvard University Press, 1921. Also, *Royal Blossom,* Translated by Aristides E. Phoutrides. New Haven: Yale University Press, 1923. And, *A Man's Death.* Translated by Aristides E. Phoutrides, Foreword by D. C. Hesseling. Athens, 1934.

[2]Kostes Palamas, *The Twelve Words of the Gypsy,* Translated with an Introduction by Frederic Will. Lincoln: University of Nebraska Press, 1964; also, *The King's Flute.* Translated with an Introduction by Frederic Will. Lincoln: University of Nebraska Press, 1967. And, Kostes Palamas, *The Twelve Lays of the Gypsy.* Translated, with an Introduction, by George Thomson. London: Lawerence & Wishart, 1969.

[3]See reviews of these translations by Dr. Costas Proussis in the *Greek Orthodox Theological Review* XII (1967), 208-212; and in *Balkan Studies,* VIII (1968), 214-5. Also by Dr. M. Byron Raizis in *Yearbook of Comparative and General Literature,* 18 (1969), 86-89; In *Philological Quarterly,* XLIX, 2 (April, 1970), 278-282; and in *Neo-Hellenika,* I (1970), 215-219.

Balkan Studies, XVI, No. 1 (1975), 215-219.

5

C. P. Cavafy, *Passions and Ancient Days,* New Poems Translated and Introduced by Edmund Keeley and George Savidis.
New York: The Dial Press, 1971, pp. 68.

C. P. Cavafy, *Selected Poems,* Translated by Edmund Keeley and Philip Sherrard.
Princeton, N.J.: Princeton University Press, 1972, pp. 97.

Constantine P. Cavafy (1863-1933) is one of the few modern Greek poets whose work has achieved international fame. Next to the works of George Seferis and Nikos Kazantzakis, Cavafy's major poetry has already appeared in book form in four different English translations, two French ones, one German, and one Italian. Individual pieces by this great Alexandrian artist had started appearing in the non-Greek literary press, in the original or in translation, as early as 1924, when E. M. Forster persuaded T. S. Eliot to publish «Ithaka» in his influential *Criterion.*

The unique and sophisticated blending of Hellenism and universality, personal honesty and artistic conviction that are the hallmark of Cavafy's verse has attracted poets, translators, and scholars ranging from W. H. Auden and Kimon Friar to Konstantinos Lardas and Minas Savvas, among several others. Some translators, like Mr. Friar, rendered Cavafy's Greek into a poetic English idiom which combines readability with precision. Others produced free and imaginative adaptations—remaining faithful to the spirit of the original—which they presented under the self-explanatory categories «anaplasi» and «parasyntheta». A strict philologist may wish to take issue with the liberties of some of the latter. In the English-speaking world, however, and especially in the

United States, free adaptations of foreign verse have become increasingly popular since very often the result is a beautiful and convincing poem in English. The artistic success of Robert Lowell's recent "imitations" is a telling example.

It is not my purpose to discuss here the originality and greatness of Cavafy's verse. My goal is an evaluation of the contribution of Edmund Keeley, Philip Sherrard, and George Savidis to the spreading of this Greek poet's reputation to the English-speaking public.

Generally speaking the impact of Cavafy's poetry in the literary circles of England and America began to be felt soon after the publication of Professor John Mavrogordato's British translation, *The Poem's of C. P . Cavafy* (London: The Hogarth Press, 1951). This volume which was introduced by Professor Rex Warner, received good reviews in the British and American periodical press, sold out fairly fast, and was reprinted twenty years later. Dr. Rae Dalven's first American edition, *The Complete Poems of Cavafy* (New York: Harcourt, Brace, and World, 1961)—by no means a "complete poems" edition, despite its title—introduced by the greatest living English poet, W. H . Auden, was generally received favorably, though a few critics were somehow annoyed by certain inaccuracies and the rather prosaic quality of her poetic medium. This fact, however, did not prevent the book from appearing as a paperback, shortly afterwards.

When Professor George Savidis published in 1968 the poems of Cavafy that had not been released before by the poet's heirs and literary executors, 'Ανέκδοτα Ποιήματα, *1882-1923* ('Αθήνα: "Ικαρος, 1968), the corpus of Cavafy's work was significantly enriched. The need then for a translation of these hitherto "unknown" pieces became apparent. Professors Keeley and Savidis must be commended for having answered that need with spectacular success.

C. P. Cavafy, Passions and Ancient Days (1971)—this title was found in Cavafy's own papers—is a beautifully printed and bound bilingual selection. Keeley and Savidis selected twenty-one out of the seventy-five poems of the 1968 Ikaros edition. Their artistic taste and sensitivity must be praised because they managed to translate and include most of the more significant or interesting poems. Moreover, their lucidly written, informative, and properly documented "Introduction" (14 pages long) traces with meticulous care the progress and general development of certain poems from the time they were conceived or outlined, to the time when the poet thought that they had almost reached the desired form. "In Church" (p. xi) is a good example of Cavafy's preoccupation with his art.

This thin volume contains adequate Notes explaining the historical and other allusions in the poems, and offering information about the history of individual poems. Finally, the presence of the Greek text (on opposite pages from the English) enables the reader who knows Greek to judge the quality of the translation himself, without having to take it for granted that these scholars' work does indeed do justice to the original.

To form an idea of how accurately and artistically Keeley and Savidis have rendered Cavafy into literary English, I offer here their translation of the poem «Κρυμμένα» p. 30, in its entirety, as well as Professor Minas Savvas's competent version of the same piece.

"Concealed"

From all I did and all I said
let them not search to find who I am.
An obstacle stood and transformed
the actions and manner of my life.
An obstacle stood and prevented me
many times from speaking out.
My most underserved actions
and my most concealed writings—
from these they may perceive me.
But perhaps it does not merit

such care and such effort to know me.
Later—in the more perfect society—
another created like myself
certainly will appear to act with freedom.

Minas Savvas's translation in *Chicago Review* (August, 1969),
p. 5.

"Hidden Things"

From all the things I did and all the things I said
let no one try to find out who I was.
An obstacle was there transforming
the actions and the manner of my life.
An obstacle was often there
to silence me when I began to speak.
From my most unnoticed actions
and my most veiled writing—
from these alone will I be understood.
But maybe it isn't worth so much concern
and so much effort to discover who I really am.
Later, in a more perfect society,
someone else made just like me
is certain to appear and act freely.

Keeley and Savidis's translation in *Passions and Ancient Days,*
p. 31.

A comparison of these two versions reveals that the Keeley-
Savidis one is more idiomatic, smoother, and less formal than
the other. Even their title is more suggestive than the adjective "Concealed". Although Savvas's translation reads well,
he does write "who I am", where Cavafy has ἤμουν, which
Keeley and Savidis have rendered correctly as "who I was".
Savvas prefers to render θά μέ νοιώσουν as "they may perceive
me", thus making it more conditional; whereas Keeley-
Savidis come closer to the Greek with their "will I be under-

stood," a simple reference to future time. Also Savvas's "in *the* more perfect society", is too Greek and less successful than "in *a* more perfect society", of the other two scholars who seems to be better versed in the subtleties of the languages involved.

The appearance of *Passions and Ancient Days* undoubtedly added new and valuable material to the Cavafy bibliography in English, though many a devotee of the Alexandrian poet, and especially researchers and serious scholars, would wish to see all of his recently released poems in good and reliable English translations, I am sure.

The aims of the second book, which is equally beautifully presented and printed, are considerably different and perhaps more ambitious. *C. P. Cavafy, Selected Poems* (1972), in which Professor Keeley collaborated with the British phil-hellene Dr. Philip Sherrard (with whom he had translated George Seferis's *Collected Poems, 1925-1955*, in 1967), contains *new* and improved translations of sixty-nine of the best known Cavafy poems. Thus, in a sense, this latest selection supersedes previously published translations (including earlier versions by Keeley and his associates), and offers a better text—the dream of all lovers of literature—for the benefit of the English readership all over the world.

Since the earlier volumes of Cavafy verse in English have already created a public that is greatly interested in his work, the desire of Keeley and Sherrard is understandable and legitimate. In addition to the sixty-nine poems, this slim volume contains Notes, a Biographical Note, a Bibliographical Note (selected items in English), and a Foreword. "Thermopylae," "Ithaka," "Waiting for the Barbarians," and most of Cavafy's epoch-making poems from the three traditional categories of the poet's poetic corpus—historical, philosophical, and erotic —are included in it, as had been done in *Passions and Ancient Days* as well. Referring to the need for these new translations, in their Foreword, these two scholars write: "Our realization of the need for new versions of poems already available to the

English reader arose out of a growing sense that Cavafy should be rendered in a style that is neither stilted nor artificial. Cavafy's use of language—a carefully modulated synthesis of *katharevousa* and *demotiki*—easily lends itself to mistranslation. It has become increasingly clear to us, during our work on Cavafy's poetry over the past twenty years that his voice is more natural, immediate, and even colloquial than extant translations—including our own earlier selections—would make it appear" (p. v.).

This claim is adequately supported by a careful comparison of their latest version to older ones. For example, the conclusion of "Waiting for the Barbarians," in its newest version is as follows:

> Now what's going to happen to us without them?
> The Barbarians were a kind of solution (p. 7).

Their earlier version, published in *Six Poets of Modern Greece* (New York, Alfred A. Knopf, 1961) and elsewhere, is less colloquial, less natural:

> And now, what will become of us without barbarians?
> Those people were a kind of solution (p. 32).

although it is literally closer to the Greek text. Professor Rae Dalven's rendition is even more formal and much less poetic:

> And now what shall become of us without any barbarians?
> Those people were a kind of solution (p. 19).

The word *shall* adds a pedantic touch which is alien to Cavafy's demotic diction in this particular passage. And the word *any* is certainly an addition arbitrarily expanding the meaning of Cavafy who intentionally wanted to be laconic and epigrammatic in his conclusion. The poet W. H. Auden had mistranslated this poem by making its end conditional and less direct when he wrote, "Those people *would* be a kind of solution."

A similar verbal and artistic improvement is noticeable, for instance, in the poem "Ithaka." Compare these three different versions of its famous ending, whose Greek is colloquial and quite unpretentious:

(1) And if you find her poor, Ithaca has not defrauded you.
With the great wisdom you have gained, with so much experience,
you must surely have understood by then what Ithakas mean.
(Rae Dalven, p. 37)

(2) And if you find her poor, Ithaka has not deceived you.
So wise have you become, of such experience,
that already you will have understood what these Ithakas mean.
(Keeley-Sherrard 1961, p. 37)

(3) And if you find her poor, Ithaka won't have fooled you.
Wise as you'll have become, and so experienced,
you'll have understood by then what an Ithaka means.
(Keeley-Sherrard 1972, p. 19)

Trying to remain uncomfortably close to the Greek Miss Dalven resorts, once more, to prosaic and formal expressions in English, like the verb *defrauded* in (1). Keeley and Sherrard in (2) use the more colloquial verb *deceived*. Also, their "So wise have you become" is much more idiomatic than the literal "With the great wisdom that you have gained" of (1). In (3) Keeley and Sherrard even avoid the awkward plural of *Ithakas,* and substitute for it *an Ithaka* which, in addition to being more idiomatic, implies also that there are more than one Ithakas, as is the spirit of the original.

Comparisons like the above can be made in many more cases. The result however, is always the same: the latest Keeley-Sherrard version easily supersedes, especially in achieving a poetic effect, the pioneer efforts of earlier translators and of themselves.

Both of these Cavafy volumes have been hailed as substantial literary achievements by the reviewers of the American press. No one can honestly disagree with them, although at least one (the novelist Lawrence Durrell in the *New York Times*) went perhaps a little too far in his praise of the erotic poems (i.e., "The Bandaged Shoulder") at the expense of other less personal pieces. A professional historian or philologist may perhaps object to the way Keeley and Sherrard transliterate Greek, Roman, and Byzantine names by oversimplifying their orthography. For instance, the quasi-phonetic transliterations Dimitrios (*Selected Poems,* p. 9), Antony (p. 10), Selefkidis (p. 34), Anna Komnina (p. 51), Dimaratos (p. 54), Kantakuzinos (p. 60), and so on, differ considerably from the scholarly, traditional, and perhaps better established, spellings Demetrios, Anthony, Comnena, Seleucides, Demaratos, Cantacuzene, which classical scholars and historians will recognize immediately. Moreover, the phonetic substitution of an English *i* for a Greek *n* will cause a non-erudite English reader to mispronounce these names. Dimaratos and Selefkidis will be read, by many, as Νταϊμάρατος and Σελεφκάϊντις, as experience teaches us. But this, of course, is a trifle when one thinks of the achievement of *Selected Poems* as a whole.

In their Foreword Professors Keeley and Sherrard announce that a "complete bilingual edition of the Greek poet's mature work" is forthcoming. This is good news. After the success of their collaboration on Seferis's *Collected Poems, 1924-1955,* and in view of what Keeley, Sherrard, and Savidis have accomplished in *C. P. Cavafy, Passions and Ancient Days,* and in *C. P. Cavafy, Selected Poems,* one may legitimately expect a definitive and possibly a monumental edition of the works of the great Alexandrian Greek poet.

Balkan Studies, XVI, No. 2 (1973), 395-399.

6

THE EMERGENCE OF MODERN GREEK POETRY

Modern Greek Poetry, From Cavafis to Elytis. Translation, Introduction and Notes by Kimon Friar. New York: Simon & Schuster, 1973. xx + 780 pages.

The artistic and cultural merits of Greek poetry written during the post-classical, Hellenistic, medieval, Byzantine, and Renaissance periods of European history have finally started attracting the attention of literary scholars and historians in this country, long after they had attracted German, French, British, Russian and other intellectuals and critics.

Modern and contemporary Greek verse, however, has fared much better with the English-speaking public. A number of books of modern Greek verse in English translations have been published in the last fifteen years or so, and several dozen literary and scholarly magazines have been publishing periodically Greek poetry in translation in the United States alone since the 1950s. The British magazines *Agenda* (1969) and *Modern Poetry in Translation* (1969), and the American *The Atlantic Monthly* (1955), *Chicago Review* (1969), *Micromegas* (1971), *Arion's Dolphin* (1972), *Boundary 2* (1972), and *The Literary Review* (1973) have dedicated whole issues to modern Greek poetry and literature in general. This unique phenomenon for a small country is certainly due to the high quality of this poetry, as well as to the talent, conscientious work, and personal sacrifice of its various translators. The most talented, prolific, and successful is probably Kimon Friar, translator of Nikos Kazantzakis' monumental *The Odyssey: A Modern Sequel* (1958) and of several other Greek texts, as well as the author of numerous scholarly articles, reviews, and textbooks.

In *Modern Greek Poetry* Friar has collected some 450 of the best and most representative lyrics and passages by thirty major Greek poets born up to 1912. These artists have been judiciously classed in five more or less homogeneous groups on the basis of aesthetic affinities, poetic idiosyncracies, and social ideologies. Under the heading "Forerunners and Traditionalists," Friar presents Constantine Cavafis, Angelos Sikelianos, Nikos Kazantzakis, Kostas Varnalis, Kostas Ouranis, Kostas Kariotakis, and Takis Papatsonis. Under "Traditions and Transitions" is presented the work of some less well known artists—some of whom are erudite critics as well: Alexander Baras, Alexander Matsas, Nikos Kavadhias, D. I. Antoniou, I.M. Panayotopoulos, Pandelis Prevelakis, George Sarandaris, and Andreas Karandonis. The group titled "The Turning Point and the Surrealists" offers samples of the work of George Seferis, Nicolas Calas, Andreas Embiricos, Nikos Engonopoulos, Nikos Gatsos, and Odysseus Elytis. "The Social Poets" includes lyrics by Yannis Ritsos (Greece's foremost Marxist poet), Nikos Pappas, Rita Boumi-Pappas, and Nikiphoros Vrettakos. The last category, "Religious and Existentialist Modes," presents two of the best poetesses— Melissanthi and Zoë Karelli—plus Nikos Ghavriil Pendzikis, George Themelis, and G. T. Vafopoulos.

The modern poetry expert will recognize on these lists the names of the 1963 Nobel Prize winner George Seferis, the much-translated Cavafis—five books of English translations alone so far, plus two paperback editions—the famous Kazantzakis, the often anthologized Elytis, Sikelianos, Ritsos, Gatsos, Embiricos, Engonopoulos, Vrettakos, and others whose poems have often become the subject of studies and dissertations in America and Europe. On the other hand, the reader will have the opportunity to enjoy, for the first time perhaps, impressive poems by Kariotakis, Karelli, Pendzikis, Prevelakis, Panayotopoulos, Varnalis, and others in precise and poetic translations.

What makes *Modern Greek Poetry* a unique contribution

to the field of modern verse isn't only the aesthetic pleasure that one derives from its rewarding contents. Friar has prefaced his translations by a long "Introduction" (130 pages) which is not only informative, scholarly, and extremely readable, but also covers the historical background, the various "schools" and tendencies, and each of the thirty artists in short but critically incisive individual chapters. That part of this book alone could constitute a valuable volume in itself if it were published separately. It contains insightful observations, brilliant commentaries, and erudite comparisons with the masters of the modern Anglo-American and European poetic tradition to which these sophisticated and cosmopolitan Greeks belong. This is necessary for the proper appreciation of these poems by non-Greek readers.

Many of these artists are polyglot scholars and critics as well; some have even translated most competently into Greek many of the greatest French, British, American, German, Italian, Spanish, Russian, and other stars in the genre ever since the era of Baudelaire.

Most of what Friar writes is refreshingly original and compares most favorably with whatever has been published on these writers by erudite specialists in Greece and elsewhere. The translations are preceded by the introductory material and the critical apparatus and are followed by Friar's fascinating professional observations on the art and science of translating verse, by biographical and bibliographical entries on all these poets and in all languages, plus explanatory notes to allusions and references in the poems, an index, and a selective bibliography of texts, translations, and secondary sources in English and in Greek. In other words, this anthology—done with loving care and scholarly method over a period of twenty years—is complete and easy to use. Readers, students, and researchers must feel at home with it since nothing seems to be missing from its pages. As a matter of fact, scholar-anthologists could use it as a model for emulation.

Friar argues persuasively about the exclusion of the celebrated Kostis Palamas (1859-1943) from his selection. Palamas certainly can be viewed as the last, and greatest, link in the poetic tradition initiated by Dionysios Solomos (1798-1857), the National Poet of modern Greece *par excellence*. Still, since Palamas is a contemporary of Sikelianos and an innovator beyond Solomos' range and scope, his absence is deeply felt. Again, one may argue that Palamas' verse doesn't offer itself readily to translation. The glaring failures of the various Palamas renditions into English (by Aristides Phoutrides, Frederic Will, George Thomson, and others) have perhaps persuaded this sensitive and perspicacious poet-translator to avoid doing a dubious service to the memory of Palamas.

To most non-Greek readers Constantine Cavafis (1863-1933)—spelled Cavafy by himself and most other translators—is the really first modern and innovative Greek poet, whose influence has been profoundly felt during the last two generations despite the fact that this Alexandrian Greek didn't establish a well-defined "school" of modern verse. Imitators of his dry wit and dramatic style are, as always, plentiful. Friar offers a generous chunk (23 poems) of Cavafis' poetic corpus composed from 1893 to 1915. "Candles," "Waiting for the Barbarians," "Thermopylae," "Ithaca," and Lawrence Durrell's favorite, "The Bandaged Shoulder"—some of his most famous pieces—offer the reader an opportunity to appreciate Cavafis at his best. The last stanza of the strikingly frank erotic "The Bandaged Shoulder" has been rendered—

> When he had gone I found beside the chair
> a bloodstained piece of cloth from the bandages,
> a rag that should have been cast out at once
> among the rubbish, but which I brought to my lips
> and kept as keepsake for a long time—
> the blood of love upon my lips.   (p. 151)

For comparison's sake, here is the same passage as translated by Professors Edmund Keeley and Philip Sherrard, Cavafis' "authorized" translators:

When he left, I found, in front of his chair,
a bloody rag, part of the dressing,
a rag to be thrown straight into the garbage;
I put it to my lips
and kept it there a long while—
the blood of love against my lips.

(In *Passions and Ancient Days*, p. 55)

This competent version, though not more faithful to the meaning of the Greek than Friar's, has been rendered in slightly more irregular lines and rhythms than those of the original. One should perhaps mention here that Mr. Friar has tried successfully to keep Cavafis' metrical schemes, from the strict metrics in the early period to his loosening of them later, and to his adoption of free verse in his final phase.

Kazantzakis' verse is represented by eleven beautiful excerpts from his colossal (33,333 lines) *The Odyssey: A Modern Sequel*, a poem perhaps destined to revitalize the epic genre in our epoch of short lyrics; two of his *terza rima* cantos, "Nietzsche" and "Buddha," plus passages from his lyrical prose of *The Saviors of God*—Kazantzakis's philosophical credo and, in a sense, *apologia pro vita atque arte sua*.

None of the celebrated and greatly cherished poems of the other artists is missing, either. The much-translated and often discussed "The King of Asine" by Seferis is there in all its glory, along with nine other major pieces by him, covering his most productive period, 1933-1953. The cryptic *Amorghos* by Gatsos, and parts of Ritsos' *Romiosini* (Greekness) are also there. Seferis' "Helen," Elytis' "Helen," "Persephone" by Karelli, "Orion" by Embiricos, "Helen" and "Eumenides" by Panayotopoulos, and "Centaur" by Baras are among the few poems in which these modern Greeks utilize, quite originally and most imaginatively, echoes from the cultural

216

heritage of their ancient nation. Their handling of classical Greek mythology will remind the reader of the degree of originality and sophistication found in foreign poems such as W. B. Yeats's "Leda and the Swan," Valéry's "Helen," or René Char's "Evadne." In terms of modern and elaborate techniques, most of these writers use allusions and symbols with the dexterity of the established masters. Seferis, in my opinion, equals T. S. Eliot in his handling of "objective correlatives" in "Helen" or "The King of Asine" and elsewhere. At the same time Seferis succeeds in sounding quite profound and erudite without burdening his verse with excessive amounts of vague, esoteric, and cryptic borrowings from abroad.

The feeling of emptiness that one feels upon the contemplation of the passing of time and the vanity and futility of all ancient and modern grandeur has been suggested most expertly by Seferis through his allusion to the Homeric King of Asine (*Iliad,* II), now only a distant and vague echo, and the hollow funeral mask of gold that covers the void that once was a mighty ruler:

> The King of Asine a void under the mask
> everywhere with us, everywhere with us, under a name:
> "'Ασίνην τε. . . 'Ασίνην τε. . ."
> . . . .
> a void under the mask.   (p. 304)
> And the poet looks at the stones and lingers, asking
>   himself
> . . . .
> image of a form turned to stone under the sentence of
>   a bitterness everlasting,
> the poet a void.   (p. 305)

The last, and one of the youngest poets in this anthology, is Odysseus Elytis. His work went through stages influenced by French symbolism and surrealism, until he found his own personal poetic idiom and style in poems like *Axion Esti*

(Worthy It Is), his great secular oratorio, and other lyrics of striking verbal originality and of idealistic inspiration. The "Gloria" part of Elytis' major opus concludes as follows:

Now to the still incurable melanosis of the moon
Aye to the Galaxy's gold-glittering azure sheen

Now to the amalgam of peoples and the Black Number
Aye to the statue of Justice and the Great Staring Eye

Now to the humiliation of the gods Now to the ashes
of Man
Now Now to Nothingness
     and Aye to the small world, the Great!   (p. 619)

These lines radiate Elytis's philosophical preoccupation with the eventual triumph of the forces of good and light over those of evil and darkness in the real cosmos. For Elytis the hour of affirmation has come: it is now.

The contents of this volume vindicate Friar's reputation as a poet-translator with exquisite taste and admirable method. At the same time it proclaims to the English-speaking public that modern Greek poetry is of high quality indeed and deserves attention and study. The Greek-speaking people never really ceased composing and enjoying lyric and epic poetry, not even during the so-called Dark Ages in the West. True, the verse of these long centuries was no match to that of Homer, Pindar, Sappho, Alkaios, Anakreon, or Simonides. To some extent, however, a similar phenomenon can be observed in the literature of Italy, England, Spain, Portugal, or Germany. Virgil and Dante haven't been equaled yet, nor have Shakespeare, Cervantes, Camoëns, Goethe and others in the rest of Europe.

It is known that Kimon Friar has already prepared an equally impressive anthology of another thirty newer and recent Greek poets, which will appear as a complement to this volume under the title, *Contemporary Greek Poetry*. On the basis of what *Modern Greek Poetry* is and has achieved, one may legitimately expect the second volume to be a most promising and valuable contribution to recent world literature.

Before concluding the presentation of this beautifully printed, bound, and organized book, one must praise and compliment Michael Korda, of Simon and Schuster, for his own excellent literary taste and willingness to produce such a rich and rewarding volume. Kimon Friar's *Modern Greek Poetry* is an all-encompassing and monumental collection which will not be superseded for decades.

Temple University, *Journal of Modern Literature,* IV, No. 1 (September, 1974), 159-163.

7

Odysseus Elytis, *The Sovereign Sun: Selected Poems,*
Translated with an Introduction and Notes by Kimon
Friar.
Philadelphia: Temple University Press, 1974, pp. 200.

Odysseus Elytis, *The Axion Esti,* An Iternational
Poetry Forum Selection, Translated by Edmund Keeley
and George Savidis.
Pittsburgh: University of Pittsburgh Press, 1974, pp.
xv + 159.

The poetry of Odysseus Elytis is not unknown to the Greekless reader of modern verse, for its first translations into
French, English, German, Italian, Spanish and other languages—in book form as well as in literary periodicals—
started appearing right after the Second World War. The
simultaneous publication of the above two volumes will, no
doubt, generate more interest in his work. Moreover, the
quality of the translations and the calibre of scholarship and
savvy that went into the making of these beautiful books, may
well result in earning for this Greek poet a place on the modern
international Parnassus right next to those occupied by Cavafy, Kazantzakis, and Seferis—the only modern Greek poets
who are well known in the English-speaking world.

My statement implies no attempt at evaluating Elytis's work
by means of comparing, or contrasting, it to the poetry of any
of the other three. Odysseus Alepoudhélis—Elytis is his pen
name—was born in Crete, in 1911. When he got his first
poems published in an issue of *Nea Ghrammata* (1935), Cavafy had already been dead for two years, Seferis was publishing
his third book of verse since 1931, and Kazantzakis was a
well-known (though always controversial) literary figure.

Like George Seferis, Elytis in his youth became acquainted with the work of the French poets of the modern tradition and especially the surrealists. Unlike Seferis, he was never attracted by the irony of Laforgue, the malaise of Baudelaire and the other "damned" poets, or the nebulous symbolism of Mallarmé—elements which probably account for Seferis's later change of course toward the direction of T. S. Eliot. Initially influenced by Paul Eluard (whose poems he has translated into Greek), because he preferred his delicate handling of surrealist expression and imagery to André Breton's rougher automatic writing, Elytis eventually developed a poetic style and idiom uniquely his own.

In terms of thematic preoccupations and concerns as well Elytis was averse to the prevalent poetic modes in his youth: he had no use for the morbid pessimism of Kostas Karyotakis, the dry irony and detachment of Cavafy, or the stoic acceptance and Olympian intellectualism of Seferis. Similarly, grand-scale expression of socio-political ·cosmotheory in verse— Kazantzakis's preoccupation—had no place at all in Elytis's lyricism, in a poetry that was "pure", yet not in the aesthetic sense that Mallarmé and Valéry implied in their definitions and practice of "poésie pure".

Elytis's pure lyricism—full of Dionysian impulses, dynamism, but no dogma—needed a special setting and a number of characters for its animation. The Greek milieu (land, sea, and sky) provided the setting of his verse: the luminous Aegean sea, the cerulean aura, the pastel hues tainting islands and shores, the ever bright and hot sun of Greece—the Sovereign Sun—and the half-naked close-to-nature lads and maidens of his youth's memories, playing, suffering, loving, and living against this dream-like and idyllic landscape of the mind, whose origin was actual reality "distanced" by the lapse of time and the moving from the world of innocence into the darker realm of experience.

This kind of lyricism characterized Elytis's earlier poetry. Kimon Friar, in his detailed and penetrating 40-page "Introduction" to *The Sovereign Sun,* discusses brilliantly the cultural backgrounds, growth, and evolution of Elytis' poetics and poetry. In his excellent poetic translations of some seventy short and long (book length) lyrics, Friar presents to the English readership abundant samples from all of Elytis's phases in his long and distinguished career as a poet. Friar's selection is organized chronologically—as it should be—and contains perhaps the best specimens from each of the poet's books or collections: *Orientations* (1939), *The Concert of Hyacinths, In the Service of Summer, Sun the First* (1943), *Heroic and Elegiac Song...* (1945), *Axion Esti* (1959), *Six and One Remorses for the Sky* (1960), *Villa Natacha* (1973), *Death and Resurrection of Constandinos Paleologhos* (1971), *The Light Tree and the Fourteenth Beauty* (1971), *The Monogram* (1971), and the couplets of *The Sovereign Sun* (1971). The editor and translator completed this admirable volume with explanatory notes (pp. 179-87), and a Greek and foreign bibliography of Elytis' texts, editions, translations, and the critical commentary that they have inspired in various languages (pp. 191-5).

Most of Elytis's titles give a good idea of how skillfully he employs surrealism in his lyric utterance. For instance, the phrase "concert of hyacinths"—despite its superficial strangeness—implies that flowers (hyacinths) can play music, which is an extremely beautiful and very poetic idea, although its verbal expression challenges momentarily our logic. An idea of Elytis's favorite imagery, with its ubiquitous touch of disciplined surrealism, may be communicated by means of the following two very different stanzas from "Beautiful Girl in the Garden" and the end of "The Sovereign Sun," respectively:

> High up with your morning delight
> Filled with the grasses of the East
> Filled with birds for the first time heard
> Oh how beautiful you are
> Casting the waterdrop of day
> On the beginning of the trees' song! (p. 71).

and
> and high up on our lookout mast we keep for sentry one
> who ever and anon remains our Sun our Sovereign Sun!
> (p. 175)

Genuine and profound joy often emanates from Elytis's lyrics, but the reader shouldn't be misled into assuming that this poet's work is facile, pretty, light and simple, full of nature descriptions and warm feelings verging on the sentimental. Friar's careful selection shows Elytis's sophistication as an artist and thinker in works like the lyrical prose of "Death and Resurrection of Constandinos Paleologhos" and the early "The Concert of Hyacinths", or the symphonic complexity of the long and moving "Heroic and Elegiac Song for the Lost Second Lieutenant of the Albanian Campaign".

Elytis's astonishing originality as a composer of poetry whose roots extend deeply into the cultural consciousness of Hellenism is not manifested only in lyrics whose subject-matter has been provided by medieval or modern Greek history. His greatest *opus* to this day is, undoubtedly, the long secular oratorio *Axion Esti* (Worthy It Is) (1959), whose intricate and complex form, metrics, and meaning are insight-fully explained by Kimon Friar ("Introduction" pp. 25-30) and represented by one dozen autonomous pieces from its main parts and their subdivisions: Genesis, Psalms, Odes, Prophetic, and Gloria—types and genres found in Byzantine devotional poetry and hymnography.

The Axion Esti can be viewed—without losing one's sense of proportion, of course—as contemporary man's carefully thought-out and splendidly executed equivalent to Beethoven's magnificent *Ninth Symphony* (Choral). Popularized by the appropriate music that Mikis Theodorakis composed to suit its Protean moods, tones, and themes *The Axion Esti* does uplift today's sophisticated connoisseur of esoteric verse in perhaps the same way that Schiller's jubilant and idealistic "Ode to Joy" (An die Freude) uplifted Beethoven and myriads of romantic souls ever since its composition.

The significance and striking originality of this impressive poetic sequence enabled the director of the International Poetry Forum to include *The Axion Esti* in its excellent series. They also inspired Tasso and Jane Katselas and the Greek Orthodox Archdiocese of North and South America to support its publication with special grants. The task of translating, annotating, editing, and presenting was undertaken by Professors Edmund Keeley and George Savidis. As was the case before, Keeley and Savidis achieved their goal with distinction.

The greatest asset of the Keeley-Savidis book of Elytis's poetry is its bilinguality—Greek and English texts printed clearly on facing pages. This enables the reader who knows Greek to compare the translation to the original and reach his own conclusion as to its value. The two editors' short preface and notes (a total of ten pages) provide some assistance to the reader of this poem. Since, however, *The Axion Esti* is here in its entirety (The Genesis, The Passion, and the Gloria with all their parts and counterparts) apparently Keeley and Savidis did not feel the need to provide an analysis of its structure as elaborate and extensive as the one offered by Kimon Friar in his edition.

The best brief but telling description of this poem, as well as a statement of its theme, can be found on the cover of the book. I quote: "Though the poem can perhaps be understood best as a spiritual autobiography which dramatizes the national and philosophical extensions of a highly personal sensibility, it is also read as an expression of the revolutionary spirit of Greece. *The Axion Esti* mirrors man's merciless struggle against the powers of darkness as the poet gives to an imaginary Christian liturgy a context which is revolutionary from several aspects besides the religious: the social, the aesthetic, and the philosophical".

Since it is far better to experience poetry rather than describe or summarize it, I wish to complete this presentation with a characteristic passage from the fifth Ode of "The Passion", quoted in the original in the Friar as well as in the Keeley-Savidis versions:

Ἑκατόγχειρες νύχτες   * μές στό στερέωμα ὅλο
Τά σπλάχνα μου ἀναδεύουν * Αὐτός ὁ πόνος καίει
Ποῦ νά βρῶ τήν ψυχή μου * τό τετράφυλλο δάκρυ!

Μέ τό λύχνο τοῦ ἄστρου   * στούς οὐρανούς γυρίζω
Στό ἀγιάζι τῶν λειμώνων   * στή μόνη ἀκτή τοῦ κόσμου
Ποῦ νά βρῶ τήν ψυχή μου * τό τετράφυλλο δάκρυ!

Nights with a hundred hands stir my entrails
Throughout the firmament. This pain burns.
How can I find my soul, the four-leaf tear!

With the star's lamp I roam the heavens.
In the frost of the meadows, the world's only shore,
How can I find my soul, the four-leaf tear!

(Keeley-Savidis, pp. 62-3)

and

Nights with a hundred arms * in the vast firmament
  Set my entrails astir   * This agony burns me
Where I might find my soul * that four-leaf teardrop!
With the lamp of the star   * I went out to the skies
  In the meadow's chill air * on the earth's only shore
Where I might find my soul * that four-leaf teardrop!

(Friar, p. 107)

It is difficult to say which of the two translations is better. Perhaps it all depends one one's artistic sensitivity or taste. At times Kimon Friar renders things more accurately and very eloquently; but at other times Edmund Keeley and George Savidis succeed in sounding quite poetic while still being precise and idiomatic. In terms of approximating Elytis's style and various forms, however, Friar seems to be "il miglior fabbro"—to echo Dante and T. S. Eliot here.

Balkan Studies, XVII, No. 1 (1976), 164-167.

225

8

Y٬nnis Ritsos, *The Fourth Dimension: Selected Poems of Yannis Ritsos*. Translated by Rae Dalven. Boston: David R. Godine, 1977. Pages xxiv, 156.

This beautifully-printed paperback is adorned by two magnificent photos of Yannis Ritsos. Greece's greatest lyric poet of Marxist persuasions, and, according to writers like Louis Aragon and Pablo Neruda, a poetic phenomenon in today's world literature.

Ritsos is the most prolific poet of our times with close to fifty volumes of creative writing to his credit ever since the epoch-making *Tractors* (1934) and *Epitaphios* (1936). Thus Dr. Rae Dalven, retired English professor and veteran translator from the Greek, had a tremendous task of selection. She seems to have solved it by primarily including in her book choice samples from twelve collections or long poems of Ritsos, which have been presented in chronological sequence. This way the careful reader may follow the artistic development of the poet over the last four decades. The contents are selections from: *Notes in the Margin of Time* (1938-41), *Parentheses* (1946-7), *The Blackened Pot* (1949), *Exercises* (1950-60), *The Moonlight Sonata* (1956), *The Window* (1960), *Beneath the Shadow of the Mountain* (1962), *Testimonies A* (1963), *Ismene* (1972), *Twelve Poems for Cavafy* (1974), and *The Wall in the Mirror* (1974).

Though some of these lyrics were translated into English and published by others, Dr. Dalven's selection complements, rather than antagonizes, the work of the other translators of Ritsos (Nikos Stangos, N. Germanacos, M. Savvas, Th. Maskaleris, Paul Merchant, Amy Mims, and, of course, Kimon Friar) as it rather adds more lyrics to the already translated number. Moreover, the translator has written a most informative "Preface," where the personal history of the man Yannis Ritsos and of his poetry is traced in adequate detail within the artistic, political, and social climate that has prevailed in Greece since the 1930s.

The person who feels empathy with Ritsos's poetic utterance will notice certain salutary developments in the quality of his recent lyricism, a certain softening of voice, a lowering of tone perhaps. His calm-inspiring "Serenity," from the 1974 collection *The Wall in the Mirror,* reads as follows in Miss Dalven's honest rendition:

> He slept serenely throughout the night
>   with the vigilant consciousness
> of his serenity—not to desire, not to
> think; his body
> stretched comfortably in the warm void
>   as if erect. At dawn
> still asleep, he heard the broom sweeping up the
>   cigarette
> butts in the ward, time, paper bags, olive pits,
> leaving behind only some red vapors and a white
>   handkerchief.
> The world is young with very light, paper flakes
> made of torn poems and torn flags.

9

Yannis Ritsos, *Chronicle of Exile,* Translated and with an Introduction by Minas Savvas. Foreword by Louis Aragon.
San Francisco: Wire Press, 1977, 93 pages.

If the English or American reader expresses disbelief at octogenarian Louis Aragon's assertion that "The Greatest Living Poet Is Named Yannis Ritsos"—in No. 1378, March 1971, of *Les Lettres Françaises*—he has but to read this slim and attractive book of Ritsos lyrics translated and introduced by his friend Professor Savvas.

I wouldn't call the *Chronicle of Exile* an anthology, for it is too short to be one; nor a collection, for it presents pieces from six different collections, including six poems in the original (three holographed in Ritsos's own Greek calligraphy), and six powerful India-ink illustrations by the poet, too. The "Translator's Introduction" (pp. 13-19) is brief but quite penetrating and analytical—not merely historical as in other books—as Dr. Savvas, himself a well-published poet in both languages, insightfully explains Ritsos's evolving technique or professional mannerisms. That is why I would call this book of lyrics a "sampler" of Ritsos art, for it gives us the flavor of his lyricism at its best, and assists us in understanding and appreciating the artist and his creation.

Professor Savvas avoided all long and polemic, narrative or doctrinaire poems of the Monemvasian bard of Romiosyne, and concentrated his efforts at selecting and translating shorter pieces from the following volumes or collections: *Chronicles of Exile, The Wall in the Mirror, Testimonies, Smoked Earthen Pot, Corridor and Stairs,* plus *Summer Preparatory School*—texts that cover the period from the turbulent 1948 to the relaxed present.

Yannis Ritsos's lyric power can be experienced in all the depth and breadth of its humanistic simplicity in short, economic, Laconic poems like the one titled "Fundamental Difference," as Dr. Savvas has rendered it:

> In the middle of the road they got hungry. They sat
>   down for their lunch,
> there, near the grass. A feather from a passing bird fell
>   on their bread. One of them
> saw it and was astonished. He stopped. The other
> continued to eat voraciously. There they separated.
>
> (p. 90)

Is this the utterance of a man who had been savagely persecuted for his social and political ideology? Or is it a profound testimony of man's capacity to remain human even under the most adverse conditions? We are deeply touched by Ritsos's naked and simple truths, and we must thank the translator for enabling the English-speaking people to see, hear, and feel them. The book has a symbolic sketch on the cover, and a fine picture of the poet on its back.

Greek World, (November-December, 1977), 42.

10

Yannis Ritsos, *Scripture of the Blind,* Translated from
the Greek, With an Introduction, by Kimon Friar and
Kostas Myrsiades.
Columbus: Ohio State University Press, 1979. 252 pages.

Takis Sinopoulos, *Landscape of Death: The Selected
Poems of Takis Sinopoulos,* Translated from the Greek,
with an Introduction, by Kimon Friar.
Columbus: Ohio State University Press, 1979. 288 pages.

With these two handsome bilingual volumes Kimon Friar
scored two new firsts in English Neohellenica. The poetry of
Dr. Sinopoulos appears for the first time in book form in
English; and a whole Ritsos collection, not yet published in
his country, appears bilingually in the United States. This
rare phenomenon had occurred longer than half a century
ago when Kostes Palamas had his *Dhilí kai Sklirí Stíh.*
published for the first time by the Neohellenic Mercury in
Chicago.

Scripture of the Blind consists of one-hundred and twelve
short poems written in an intense two month period from 28
September to 28 November 1972, when the Junta miasma had
started to have a corrosive effect on creative intellectuals who
like Greeks from all walks of life, could foresee no end to it.
The completion of the final draft by 1 January 1973 in Athens
long after the poet's release from detension, due to inter
national protests, occurred before the tragic events at th
Athens Polytechnic in November of that year. This is impor
tant because it helps us understand and appreciate the grave
if not pessimistic, tone and depressed, almost hopeless, atmo
sphere that pervade these lyrics and distinguish them from

pre-April 1967 or post-July 1974 compositions that express substantially different attitudes of Ritsos *vis-à-vis* the condition of his beloved Romiosyne.

Friar and Myrsiades have written a fifteen-page Introduction, one page of Notes, and a two-page biographical sketch through 1978. The student and the reader of Ritsos thus have the details and facts that are necessary for their appreciation of this book as an integral part of his enormous literary output to this day.

The introductory essay is, at the same time, comprehensive and specific in its discussion of scope, themes, technique, recurrent images and motifs. Almost surrealistic at a first reading, these pieces are actually records and photographs, or rather negatives, of nightmares caused by traumatic experiences, and of observations of objects in casual or strange relations to real, but vaguely described, persons. The narrative, mostly descriptive, sounds superficially incoherent with juxtapositions of opposites and associations of the seemingly unrelated in an incremental enumeration of images that provoke a powerful emotional response to the reader and, no doubt, a cathartic release to the poet. "Full of strange imminense," writes Mr. Friar, "*Scripture of the Blind* is a world of the monstrous and the strange, a world filled with a vague expectation of the arrival of someone or something" (p. xxiv).

Material objects (pots, knives, boxes, mirrors, tables, chairs, walls, rooms etc.) interact with living and dead people (more than four score in all) to conceptualize the passive and pathetic drama that in Ritsos's panoramic memory created specific scenes of extraordinary intensity and evocative power. Several poems are analyzed in detail (e.g., "Poetry," "At the Harbor's End," and "Outline of a Nightmare") thus enabling the reader to understand *how* and perhaps *why* the mute sing and communicate, the blind see and foresee, the dead act and suffer. The surrealistic aspect of the poems is then toned down, and their imagistic quality is properly understood as a quite different device to what we have experienced in the work

231

of, say Amy Lowell and other world poets, who drew pictures in words to substitute them as stimuli for desired emotional reactions. In Ritsos's verse words are the images, the metaphors, the agents of a dramatic instance under scrutiny, or as Mr. Friar put it: "They are individual and isolated dots of a Braille system that must be read by the groping fingers of all the senses to make out the holy scripture of the blind" (p. xxii).

"Liturgical" (p. 63), a poem brilliantly discussed by the translators, is a good example of Ritsos's technique as well as of the multiplicity of possible meanings despite its brevity:

> He placed the paper box on the table quietly
> as though it were a closed, uninhabited monastery. For a while
> he was gone in the other room. We could hear the faucet running—
> perhaps he was washing his hands with soap. On returning,
> he opened the box with great care and placed
> his left hand within it. Then with his right hand
> he grasped his left by the wrist, took it out,
> raised it up high, and showed it to us.

Its simple, descriptive opening makes it clear that the hands, not the person, are the protagonists of this particular scene. By the middle of the poem we begin to suspect a symbolic meaning which is suggested by the title that implies some kind of a ritual, and by the simile likening the box to a "Closed, unihabited monastery." The editors do not insist on a specific interpretation, since the poet preferred to leave it "open" and rich in suggestive innuendoes. Parallelly to the insightful reading of the translators, which is based on cultural and folk-loric observations, one who knows Ritsos's Marxist ideology may offer a political exegesis based on the opposite adjectives *right* and *left* which qualify the two "actors," the man's hands. The man placed his washed left hand into the strange "sanctum" of that symbolic box. But immediately his right hand (with all its connotations as correct, proper, legitimate, agile etc.) seized it firmly and demonstrated it to the vaguely-defined spectators, "us." These ritualistic gestures may be taken as a metaphor of how the Right and the Left function within the Greek body politic (the man). One could even venture to say that the Right "forces" the Left to be shown when and how it so desires.

The fact that the Greek and the English texts are printed *en face,* on opposite pages, also helps the reader realize how Mr. Friar works as a translator. We are told that Dr. Myrsiades did the first, literal, translation, and added suggested synonyms and alternates. Mr. Friar then assumed the difficult task of turning that "working text" into a literary one, good poetry in English. In the process some words, idioms, grammatical tenses or numbers, and syntactical structures or order, undergo creative alterations and become a true poem in the target language. Then the translator discusses these changes with the poet, who knows English, and accepts the suggested change, or further works with Mr. Friar until a happy and final compromise is reached. When in a few instances a critical reader may feel that a particular rendition is a bit too free, or even inaccurate, or unwarranted by the context—as I felt on some occasions—he should bear in mind that this poetic English text has Yannis Ritsos's approval.

Scripture of the Blind is a beautiful and valuable book, indeed. Kimon Friar and Professor Myrsiades have offered a new dimension to our awareness of Ritsos's ambience. The Publisher, however, must be censured for his inexcusable refusal to send galley proofs to the two editors for corrections —despite Mr. Friar's urgent and repeated requests—because a number of silly errors that unavoidably were made during the three transcriptions of the translation, would have been undoubtedly seen and corrected, and this fine volume would have been totally unblemished and perfect.

Takis Sinopoulos is a man of many talents, like Yannis Ritsos. A medical doctor who served with the Greek Army in 1940-41 and during the Civil War, Sinopoulos is a known poet, a successful painter, an astute critic, and an active supporter of democratic developments in often turbulent and tragic Greece. There is no doubt that Mr. Friar's fine translation of a generous and excellent selection of his verse will properly introduce English-speaking poetry lovers to his most original and powerful work.

Landscape of Death is prefaced by a long and brilliant Introduction in several chapters (some thirty-six pages). The Greek and English texts, always *en face,* are followed by a sixteen-page Appendix analyzing and explaining leitmotifs. A brief biography, a bibliography of Greek editions, and nine pages of Notes complete this attractive and scholarly book. The material in the *apparatus criticus* has also appeared in Greek, under the same telling title, as a critical monograph of over one-hundred pages, published by Kédhros.

More than sixty short, medium, and long poems from the collections *Midpoint* (1951), *Cantos I-XI* (1953), *Acquaintance with Max* (1956), *Midpoint II* (1957), *Helen* (1957), *Night and Counterpoint* (1959), *The Song of Ioanna and Konstandinos* (1961), *The Poetry of Poetry* (1964), *Stones* (1972), *Deathfeast* (1972), and *The Chronicle* (1975) represent here the impressive poetic corpus of Dr. Sinopoulos.

Like Ritsos, Sinopoulos is also a product of his times, of our criminal and absurd age of brutality and spiritual desolation. The horrors of the Second World War, the Occupation, the fratricidal conflict that followed them, and the inner, personal and social,traumas they caused made Sinopoulos see the setting of his adventurous existence as a "landscape of death"—a phrase he so aptly coined in his, by now classic, lyric "Elpenor." With the exception of *Acquaintance with Max*—where Max's persona as Mr. Friar observes "is, in short, one aspect of Sinopoulos during an interval in his life when he was himself brimming in ecstatic concord with the world" (p. xviii)—the poet returned faithfully to his world view as a hopeless and depressing waste land, peopled by ghosts of slain and dead companions, lost and forgotten loves, and associated with recurrent images and instances of horror.

Unlike Ritsos, however, who faced the personal and social adversities in life armed with his militant and, consequently, optimistic ideology, Sinopoulos did not particularize the burning issues, putting the blame on Right or Left, but faced them as a metaphysical thinker, as manifestations of the general moral dereliction in the contemporary world. Thus, on the contrary, Sinopoulos generalized and even universalized his pessimistic or negative outlook. The men and women in the dramas of his poems—Madga, Ioanna, Helen, Prosoras, Lukas, Alafouzos *et al.*—are at the same time intimate relations or haunting memories and echoes, while they also enact a broader drama in which they function almost like the persons one encounters in the "private" narratives of confessional poems—they weave the fabric of a myth, a fable that can tell the story of our times with as many known common denominators as a tortured memory can retain.

Not a political writer, Dr. Sinopoulos is a modern romantic, as Mr. Friar calls him, who is obsessed with the darkness that dims or colors his vision—a vision he would have liked to have been idyllic and Edenic. He is also pained by the bright light that, strangely, instead of suggesting the positive and life-giving presence of the sun—the glorious "Sovereign Sun" according to Odysseus Elytis—acts as a negative force burning and torturing with its spear-like rays, casting light on what had better remain in darkness, and illumining a Dantean milieu of hellish grotesqueness.

Extremely useful is Mr. Friar's discussion of recurrent motifs—memory, night and darkness, the dead, loneliness, silence, shouts, the sun, fire and flame, burning, and light—most of which are interrelated, and interact as elements that energize and control the articulation of Sinopoulos's tormented vision. Love, in all its dimensions, doesn't seem to have a redeeming quality, or one that lasts long, in the poet's consciousness, probably because of the transitoriness of its factors, the human beings, and their idiosyncratic behavior that often turns marriage and companionship into a nightmare of mutual agony, unilateral tyranny, or further sorrow and anguish, as we see in *The Song of Ioanna and Konstandinos* and several shorter pieces.

The best poem to introduce the reader to Dr. Sinopoulos's achievement is, perhaps, "Elpenor," whose opining lines set the tone, mood, setting, and feature the leitmotifs that reappear in many subsequent and important pieces (p. 5):

> Landscape of death. Sea turned to stone, black cypress trees,
> low seashore ravaged by salt and light,
> hollow rocks, the implacable sun above them,
> and neither the water's rolling nor a bird's wing,
> only an endless, dense, unwrinkled silence.

Motivated by his painful experiences, inspired by a Greek translation of Ezra Pound's *Canto I* (which is a liberal transcription of the Homeric *Odyssey* XI), and echoing Seferian mannerisms, especially from "The King of Asine" and his own "Elpenor," on purpose, to exploit their cultural implications as allusions of sorts, Sinopoulos concludes his lyrical and suggestive narrative:

> The sea, the cypress trees, the seashore petrified
> in deadly immobility. And only he, Elpenor,
> for whom we had sought with so much patience in old
>   manuscripts,
> tormented by the bitterness of his perpetual loneliness,
> the sun falling in the empty spaces of his thoughts
> as he dug the sand blindly with the stubs of his fingers,
> and then dwindled like a vision and slowly vanished
> in the empty, wingless, soundless, azure ether (p. 7).

The nature of this poem shouldn't make the reader assume that in the remaining pieces one finds "more of the same" in terms of technique, thematic concerns, versification, and form. On the contrary, later compositions show drastic changes in form, like in *Acquaintance with Max;* in tone, as in "Spring and Maria," or in mood, as in "Intoxication." There are also lyrics written entirely in prose-"Madga"-or in very long lines followed by shorter ones, or by prose paragraphs, as we see in the sequences titles "Nights" and "Essay." The last poem in this selection begins with the sentence, "Greece has been traveling within Greeece following the spilt and squandered blood." This travel metaphor-that somehow reminds us of Seferis's use of the same image (cf. "In the Manner of G. S.")—epigrammatically sums up the source of Sinopoulos's inspiration. Wherever he wanders he confronts man-made destruction, victims, and death. Despite the numerous changes in situations, dramatis personae, and settings, his overall impressions are those of a Dante-like traveler through a contemporary landscape of death. We must be thankful to Kimon Friar whose scholarly skills and artistic taste help to vicariously experience the honest anguish of Takis Sinopoulos in an exemplary rendition into poetic English.

11

Angelos Sikelianos, *Selected Poems.* Translated and
Introduced by Edmund Keeley and Philip Sherrard.
Princeton University Press. 1979. 152 pages.

A celebrated, dynamic, prolific, and larger-than-life personality Sikelianós (1884-1951) was the last traditional poet
of modern Greece, an artist and intellectual whose creativity
went through phases and idiosyncratic manifestations which,
at times and with certain qualifications, were somewhat
comparable to the oracular oratory of Whitman, the visionary metaphysics of Rilke, and the Dionysian impulses and
vibrations of Yeats.

Twenty-five pieces (ranging in size and form from sonnet to
lengthy lyrical compositions in metrical verse), a short introduction, notes, and a useful chronology make up this
unique contribution to the presentation of Sikelianós's impressive poetic output to anglophone readers. Some of these
translations had previously appeared in literary magazines of
quality and in an anthology; the present selection, however, is
a more systematic and representative sample of his work
despite the exclusion, of course, of passages from the powerful
verse dramas that dominated Sikelianós's last creative period.

In their penetrating introduction Keeley and Sherrard
mention the visionary quality of much of his great poetry,
as well as "the celebration of life's forms and sensual energies,"
in a kind of mystical intensity "which transcends the merely
temporal and fugitive"—as one may see in early poems like
"Return," or later ones like "Agraphon."

A believer in the unity and continuity of Hellenic civilization
from the legendary times of Homer through the mystical ages
of Byzantium and then on to the ethnic cultural expression

of modern Greece, Sikelianós chanted of nature and "the body electric," of mythic and historic heroes or divinities, of Christianty and more recent folkloric features, with the felicitous ease and conviction of a giant who encompassed and possessed all of Hellenism's spiritual legacy and could make it a genuine part of his personal bardic utterance.

Because of the complexity and bulk of his *oeuvre,* and of the colossal problems presented by his lyrical tone of voice, demotic eloquence, and exquisite harmonious effects—most of which were lost in the translation, as the two honest scholars admit—this selection is not likely to have (in my opinion) the definitiveness and impact that their previous books of Seferis's and Cavafy's poems in translation had on British and American readers. Rather than be blamed for something quite beyond their human skills Keeley and Sherrard should be praised for enabling the Greekless poetry lover to savor and enjoy lines like these from the celebrated "Thalero":

> There, as I heard the nightingale and ate fruit from the dish
>   in front of me,
> I had the taste of wheat, of song and honey
>   deep in the palate.

> Ἐκεῖ τ᾽ ἀηδόνια ὡς ἄκουγα, τριγύρα μου, καί τούς
>   καρπούς γευόμουν ἀπ᾽ τό δίσκο,
> εἶχα τή γέψη τοῦ σταριοῦ, τοῦ τραγουδιοῦ καί τοῦ μελιοῦ
>   βαθιά στόν οὐρανίσκο. . . (ππ. 32-33)

Traditional rhyme patterns cause frustration to most translators. Keeley and Sherrard will not sacrifice precision of meaning to experimentation with what might be questionable rhyme schemes in the target language. At times, however, this unwillingness to attempt an *anaplasis* of the exact original form into the same form that exists in English as its very counterpart results in rather awkward forms, like the six sonnets without rhymes and steady measures (pp. 8-19, 96-97);

or, worse still, English stanzas or units with one line less than the Greek (e.g., "Agraphon" and parts of "Artemis Orthia") where the advantages of reducing original stanzas by one line in their English rendition are not quite apparent to the reader.

SELECTED BIBLIOGRAPHY

In addition to the books presented in the REVIEWS section, the following verse translations into English deserve attention:

Constantine P. Cavafy, *The Complete Poems of Cavafy*. Expanded Edition. Translated by Rae Dalven, with an Introduction by W.H. Auden. New York: Harcourt, Brace, Jovanovich, 1976.

Constantive P. Cavafy, *Collected Poems*. Translated by Edmund Keeley and Philip Sherrard. Edited by George Savidis. Princeton, N.J.: Princeton University Press, 1975.

Yannis Ritsos, *Selected Poems*. Translated by Nikos Stangos, with an Introduction by Peter Bien. Athens: Efstathiadis Group, 1981. Reprinted from Penguin Books, 1974.

Yannis Ritsos, *Eighteen Short Songs of the Bitter Motherland*. Translated from the Greek by Amy Mims. Edited and with an Introduction by Theo. G. Stavrou. Minneapolis: The North Central P. Co., 1974.

Yannis Ritsos, *Gestures and Other Poems, 1968-70*. Translated from the Greek by Nikos Stangos. London: Cape Goliard Press, 1971.

Yannis Ritsos, *Ritsos in Parentheses*. Translations and Introduction by Edmund Keeley. Princeton, N. J.: Princeton University Press, 1979.

Yannis Ritsos, *The Lady of the Vineyards*. Translated by Apostolos Athanassakis. New York: Pella P. Co., 1979.

George Seferis, *Three Secret Poems*. Translated by Walter Kaiser. Cambridge, MA: Harvard University Press, 1969.

Takis Sinopoulos, *Selected Poems*. Translated and with an Introduction by John Stathatos. San Francisco and London: Wire Press - Oxus Press, 1980.

Resistance, Exile and Love. An Anthology of Post-War Greek Poetry. Translated and Edited by Nikos Spanias. New York: Pella P. Co., 1977.

Six Poets of Modern Greece. Chosen, Translated, and Introduced by Edmund Keeley and Philip Sherrard. New York: Alfred A. Knopf, 1961.

Twenty Contemporary Greek Poets. Edited by Dinos Siotis and John Chioles. Introduction by Nanos Valaoritis. San Francisco: Wire Press (The Coffeehouse 7-8), 1979.

Modern Greek Music and Poetry. Editor K. Mitsakis. Bilingual. Athens: Grigoris, 1979.

Manolis Anagnostakis, *The Target : Selected Poems*, Translated from the Modern Greek with an Introduction by Kimon Friar. New York: Pella, 1981.

Odysseus Elytis, *Maria Nephele : A Poem in Two Voices*, Translated from the Greek by Athan Anagnostopoulos. Boston : Houghton Mifflin Co., 1981.

Odysseus Elytis, *Selected Pems*, Chosen and Introduced by Edmund Keeley and Philip Sherrard. Translated by E. Keeley, P. Sherrard, G. Savidis, J. Stathatos, N. Valaoritis. New York : The Viking Press, 1981.

Odysseus Elytis, *Poems,* Translation with an Introduction by Nanos Valaoritis. San Francisco : Wire Press, 1982.

Kostes Palamas, *The King's Flute*, Preface by Charles Diehl and Introduction by E.P. Papanoutsos, Translated by Theodore Ph. Stephanides and George C. Katsimbalis. Athens : The Kostes Palamas Institute, 1982.

INDEX

243

245

247